Praise

'In Elaine Penhaul's latest bool   ___ __ provide
a degree of clarity to the world of home selling.
Selling your home can be a daunting experience
and it's not just about finding a buyer anymore –
it's about finding the best buyer at the best price.
Different houses need different solutions; different
agents work well for differing circumstances,
presentation and marketing are key to awareness
and desire. Taking Elaine's book in hand, you can
benefit from her many years working as one of the
preeminent home staging specialists in the UK,
backed up with industry insight and experience from
both sides of the fence. A worthy read to help any
discerning seller successfully navigate the choppy
seas of home buying and selling in the UK.'
— **Nathan Emerson**, CEO, Propertymark

'Elaine is an expert in helping us maximise the value
our clients get for their property. She understands
intimately the importance of our presentation
strategy and how the combination of maximum
presentation and exposure generates maximum
price. Her ability and understanding of property
presentation is better than many agents I know.
Read this book now if you are planning to sell in the
coming months.'
— **Daniel Harrington**, Fine & Country,
Managing Director, Global Growth

'Elaine emphasises the transformative power of preparation in selling your home. She advises homeowners to view their property through the lens of a potential buyer to maximise appeal and value to get your home sold.'
— **Christopher Watkin**, Estate Agency trainer

'This book is important. It provides the clearest plan on how to sell your house most effectively. If you are an agent or homeowner thinking of selling, this book is a must read!'
— **Simon Leadbetter**, Founder, We Are Unchained

HOW TO SELL YOUR HOUSE

The definitive guide to marketing
your biggest capital asset

ELAINE PENHAUL

Re think

First published in Great Britain in 2024 by Rethink Press
(www.rethinkpress.com)

© Copyright Elaine Penhaul

Cover image © Shutterstock | Adiyatma

For Rob, thank you. If you weren't mending the fences, I couldn't be writing the books!

Contents

Introduction

If you are selling your home or thinking about selling your home in the next few years, then this book is for you.

Selling your home can be a stressful and difficult process. It is a team game; you are the team manager and you need to decide who you want on your team. There are three distinct stages to selling a home: preparation, promotion and progression. This book focuses on the first two phases, explaining them in detail to help you achieve the best offer possible.

You will gain an understanding of basic marketing theory and how it applies to your sale. I explain the role of home staging, why you need professional photography, videography and a social media strategy to sell your home. You will learn how to find the right estate agent to help you and you will be clear about your role as a key player on team 'sell my house'.

Good preparation relies heavily on you, the seller, doing the work, with good advice and support from your chosen agent. The second stage, promotion, will mostly be done by your agent with some support from you. The third stage, progression, isn't the focus of this book, as it is usually done by a conveyancer with lots of nudging from your agent to make sure it happens in a timely fashion. You are looking for an agent who can offer great advice about how to get ready for your sale, do fantastic promotion for your property, negotiate the best price, and who will work closely with the conveyancers to make sure the sale doesn't stall.

My first book, *Sell High, Sell Fast,*[1] was published in October 2020. It became an Amazon bestseller and has opened doors for me to speak at events around the world about the benefits of staging a home before sale. It accelerated my business, Lemon and Lime Interiors, to become a leading staging business working with premium estate agents in the UK. What I have learned in the three years since its publication is that the first book didn't go far enough in communicating *all* the things a seller needs to think about to maximise their sale. In particular, it didn't explain how to work with the best estate agents, at whatever price point in the market, to get results. *How To Sell Your House* fills those gaps.

Property marketing has changed dramatically over the last fifteen years, and especially rapidly since the Covid-19 pandemic began in 2020. Houses can now be sold entirely online, via videos and virtual tours. We have seen houses being bought and sold without the buyers ever setting foot in the house before the exchange of contracts. It is possible to get a good feel for a property long before you arrive to view. The pace of change in social media has driven similarly fast changes in consumer behaviour.

What does this mean for you? Do you need to 'declutter'? Redecorate? Spend money on professional photography or a video tour? What is meant by 'home staging' and a 'virtual tour'? All these terms have entered the home-selling vernacular in the last few years. Many estate agents are struggling to clearly explain the impact of these things to their clients. Home sellers don't know what they should be asking for, or why they should be paying one agent a higher fee than another. Estate agency, at least in some quarters, has become a 'race to the bottom', with agents willing to give a high valuation and offer a low fee just to get business.

If you haven't sold recently, you probably don't know what you can and should be asking your estate agent to do. According to a Zoopla and Hometrack poll from May 2022, the average time for a homeowner to stay in their property in the UK is now twenty-three years.[2] This means that both the buyer and seller are relatively unsophisticated clients. The world of buying and selling a home has likely changed significantly since the last time you had to do it – many of our clients haven't sold a house since before Rightmove was launched. It isn't like going to the supermarket or even buying a new car. Estate agents are immersed in buying and selling homes every day. Sometimes they overlook the piece of the jigsaw where their clients need to play catch-up on the most up-to-date ways of marketing a house.

I want to help sellers understand what it takes to maximise a house sale in the UK in the digital era. The book will answer all the questions you didn't know you should be asking. I'll point you in the right direction to find the information you need in order to actively participate in getting the best sale for your home.

I have interviewed lots of experts who understand how best to sell a house today. I'll help you understand what you should be paying your estate agent to do and, crucially, how much you should be paying.

By the end of the book, you and your estate agent will become a marketing machine focused on achieving the best price for your home in record time. But if you need advice quickly, you can skip to the summary at the end of each chapter. If you have an agent coming round in the next hour or two, the Appendix has a list of dos and don'ts and some questions for you to put to the beauty parade of estate agents you invite to your home when the time comes to move.

PART ONE
PLANNING

1
Estate Agency In The Post-Pandemic World

This chapter sets out the background to the world of estate agency we are now in, and what's led us here. It explains:

- What's different about using an estate agent in 2024 compared to the last time you bought or sold a house

- What types of estate agents exist and what this means for you when you sell

- What estate agents have to do

- What estate agents may not know

- How to make sure you get the right estate agent to sell your house

How has estate agency changed?

It is unlikely that anyone moving house in the UK these days would do so without visiting Rightmove. Rightmove, started in 2000, is the largest online property portal in the UK, hosting the details of over one million homes at any one time.

Before Rightmove, estate agents largely relied on newspapers, their shop window on the high street and the Rolodex on their desk to match sellers with buyers. Homes were bought and sold by word of mouth and an estate agent could be relied upon to identify a potential buyer and talk them into booking a viewing. These days, it is entirely possible for an estate agent to have no idea that someone is looking to buy a home in their area. A would-be buyer doesn't have to speak to anyone until a property they see online piques their interest and they want to view. This means that everything listed must be able to attract potential buyers in a more passive way than has been done previously. Buyers of the Instagram generation are used to looking through social media feeds full of beautiful images and videos of carefully curated interiors. Many are not remotely interested in living in a house that doesn't already look fabulous, or in having to do the hard work of imagining how they would transform a property themselves. Your estate agent might list your house online and speak to absolutely no-one about it, in which case the presentation of your home online may be your only shop window.

When the housing market was closed on and off through the pandemic, people who needed to sell their home were thrown into a state of confusion and anxiety. Estate agents had no idea how they would stay in business and, like so many other industries, began to look at new ways to work. Multiple lockdowns meant that in-person viewings were difficult, and at times illegal. Yet the situation precipitated more people than ever suddenly wanting to move. There was a mass exodus from the cities to more rural homes that offered more space and fewer neighbours. Anyone who had ever considered moving to the countryside made a quick decision that now was the moment. House prices, even for the type of properties that had traditionally been hard to sell, rose inexorably. For the first time in living memory, rural areas saw much bigger growth, both in transactions by volume and in price increases, than London. The northwest saw the highest annual price growth, with average prices increasing by 11.2% in the year to December 2020. In the same period, the average growth in London was just 3.5%.[3]

This put huge pressure on a system that was struggling to cope. Estate agents had to adapt, and adopt new technologies and approaches. The result of these changes is that buyers have much higher expectations about what they can learn about a property before they book a viewing. For example, it has become rare to list without a floorplan, and video has become a 'must have' rather than a 'nice to have'.

Different kinds of estate agent

In response to the changing market trends that resulted from the pandemic, the traditional model of estate agency changed almost overnight. This means that now, many people who haven't sold recently are confused about the options open to them.

There are more models of estate agency than ever before. You may wonder whether this makes any difference to you as a seller. To help answer that question, I'll give you some definitions and then you can consider how these models might apply to your situation.

Corporate agent

A corporate estate agent is one that belongs to a big company and the rules are set by head office. Everyone is an employee and they are all bound by the same operating standards and processes. Examples of the corporate model would be Knight Frank and Savills in the premium market, and Connells and Spicerhaart in the middle market. The corporates tend to have a big brand name and long-established reputation behind them that will automatically attract buyers and sellers to their door.

Franchise agent

Franchising is a way for a business to operate nationally but give regional offices a degree of operational freedom under a local business owner. A franchisee will need to abide by the standards set out by head office but they have an element of individual flexibility. Examples of franchised estate agents are Newton Fallowell, Northwood, and the Belvoir Group.

Licensed or self-employed agent

This model of estate agency has grown by 500% since 2019 and self-employed agents now make up 1.8% of the total number of agents.[4] Many of these agents represent brands, such as eXp and Keller Williams, founded in the US, or The iad Group, which is European. Currently, the most widely distributed of the UK brands is Fine & Country, who operate in the premium end of the market. The self-employed agents belonging to a brand have greater freedom than a franchisee in how they operate but head office will ensure they adhere to brand guidelines, and provide training and other resources. They still benefit from having a big brand name behind them but don't have the same restrictions or upfront costs as a franchisee could have.

Independent agent

The independent agent is usually a local operator who may have one branch, or a few branches within the same geographic area. This is the traditional high street agent model. The business is usually owned by an individual or a partnership and most of the people working there are employees.

Hybrid model

A hybrid agent can offer the personal service of a local independent agent but they don't have the overhead costs of a physical office. They operate digitally and offer a low-cost fixed fee but you have a local point of contact. Yopa is probably the best-known example of the hybrid model, and they have been much more stable as a business than their fully online counterparts in the upheaval of the last few years.

Online agent

An online agent is one that only operates digitally and provides telephone support through their head office. Online agents became successful by offering a low-cost fixed fee, which is essentially a fee for listing your home on the online portals. The best known of the online agents, Purple Bricks, was sold to a newer rival in May 2023 for £1. This model of agency has suffered in the last few years; recent figures show a 33% decline in the market share of online agents since 2019.[5]

Does it matter?

Does it matter which type of model your estate agent works under? Yes and no. To some extent, it depends on the type of property you are selling and what level of service you are expecting. The biggest difference between the models is who you will be dealing with throughout the transaction and what their availability is like outside of normal office hours. Jason Bull, the head of coaching and training for The iad Group, which has recently entered the UK market, told me that in his opinion the biggest differentiator between the self-employed model and the traditional model is that you will deal with your self-employed agent consistently. The person you see at the market appraisal will be the person who does the viewings and chasing the solicitors as the sale progresses. The self-employed agent tends to take on fewer properties at once and is visible to their clients throughout the transaction.

If you are happy to do most of the work involved in selling your house yourself, you may feel that an online agent who just lists your home on Rightmove for you is the answer. If this is your choice, go in with your eyes open and still follow the advice in this book to make your listing as impactful as you possibly can.

Do you need an estate agent at all?

You might be wondering if there's a further option – using no agent at all, and doing everything yourself. This is certainly possible, people can and do achieve a sale for themselves, as the below case study shows.

CASE STUDY: The DIY estate agent

We were asked to stage a much smaller property than is the norm for our portfolio. I explained to Tom, the seller, that our service was not the cheapest option for a smaller property. He explained that he was planning to sell the house on Facebook himself. He wanted it to look amazing and knew from our reputation that he could trust us to get it right.

Tom finished the decorating and repairs he was doing himself after his tenant had moved out and the house was left empty, then we fully furnished it to appeal to a young professional couple as our target buyer. We used lots of greenery, texture and layering to reflect the current trends. We booked a professional photographer to take the pictures and Tom posted the photos straight onto Facebook. Within twenty-four hours he called us to say he had a buyer with whom he had agreed an offer at 5% over the guide price.

Clearly, in the above case, Tom didn't need the help of an estate agent to achieve his offer. It is perfectly possible to sell your home without the help of an agent. In fact it is now much easier, with the advent of social media, because you can reach a lot of potential buyers quickly. In the days before Facebook, Instagram and TikTok, the only way to sell your home yourself was to put a board outside and hope someone who wanted to buy drove past.

What exactly does an estate agent do when it comes to selling a home now? A good estate agent brings value to their clients by leveraging all the best marketing tools available to get a high offer as quickly as possible. The estate agent is the negotiator of the deal. They will act on behalf of their buyer to make sure that any offer is the best possible; they will be able to give sound advice to you, as the seller, if there are multiple offers on the table. The agent is the liaison between the buyer, the seller and their solicitors. They take responsibility for keeping things on track while the legal process is completed. This is often the most stressful part of a home sale and having an agent you trust can make a big difference.

How to decide

Ex-estate agent Simon Gates of the *Opening the Gates* podcast explained to me how home sellers can find out more about local estate agents before they decide who to instruct. Gates's first tip was to look at Google reviews. Not just at how good the reviews are but also at how consistent they are. He advises that you check the reviews are recent in case personalities have changed significantly since the last one was posted.

Gates also recommends looking at the estate agent comparison site, GetAgent. This will give you a basic comparison of estate agents in your area and their performance on metrics such as speed to sale and price achieved relative to guide price. You can also look at Rightmove and use the SSTC (sold subject to contract) filter. Comparing the number of properties an agent has listed with those that are under offer will give you a feel for how good each agent is at finding buyers. The estate agent trainer Christopher Watkin told me, 'Estate agents care more about getting listings than about selling homes.' This may be true of some, but isn't true of all. Do your homework.

Zoopla is another valuable source of information, with a filter for 'price reduced'. As Gates explained to me, if an agent typically has 40% of their listed properties showing as price reduced, you should be suspicious about whether they are valuing too high to win your business and may reduce your asking price quickly once they have it. This is not the agent you need.

Social media is another good way to find out more about any of the agents you might choose to sell your home. You can get a good sense of someone from what they post. Are they knowledgeable about the local area and the local market? Are they selling homes like yours on a regular basis? Are their listings compelling?

There are good agents in every area, you just need to find the one for you. To do this, you should:

- Check websites and social media accounts, including their LinkedIn profile.

- Look at online reviews and testimonials.

- Find properties you think are being marketed well online and use those to start the conversation with an agent about what they would do for you.

- Consider being a secret shopper – call the office and ask to book a viewing to see how this is handled.

- Check to see if they are qualified and members of any professional bodies. These are likely to be Propertymark, the Guild of Property Professionals, the Relocation Agent Network (RAN) or the Federation of Independent Agents (FIA) for residential sales agents.

- Ask what other professionals the agent works with, and how. For example, a stager, photographer and videographer. Be prepared to pay upfront for some services and consider it an investment in achieving a better sale.

- Find out what the marketing strategy will be for your home.

- Don't expect to get great marketing and great service for a cheap fee; be prepared to pay for what you need to achieve the best sale.

Qualifications

Another differentiator is training and qualifica-tions. Estate agency is currently an industry with a low bar to entry. There is no government edict that says estate agents have to hold a particular qualification. It is perhaps unsurprising then that, historically, there has been poor practice in the industry. Estate agents in the UK tend to be the butt of jokes and are not universally trusted. For many years, estate agency has featured close to the bottom of the IPSOS Veracity Index of trusted professions and, in 2023, they ranked just one place above politicians.[6] Jason Bull observes that, compared to Europeans, Brits are more willing to accept shoddy service. It is what we have become accustomed to in estate agency and, when we come to sell our homes, we seem to be resigned to it. But there are great estate agents fighting to change this perception; you just need to find yours.

I asked Russell Quirk of ProperPR, a PR business specialising in property, what he thinks is the answer to getting a better standard of estate agency in this country:

> 'I think it has to start with licensing. It is no coincidence that in markets where there's licensing, there are higher standards. There is a much better perception about agents in countries like the US and Australia. Every market that has licensing charges more than we do in the UK, and that's not a coincidence.'

So are our low service standards a case of 'you get what you pay for'? In countries where the licensing and training of estate agents is compulsory, standard fees are anything from 3–6%. The average estate agent fee in the UK is 1.42%.[7]

Is the UK licensing of estate agents likely to happen any time soon? I spoke to Timothy Douglas, Head of Policy and Campaigns at Propertymark, the leading professional body for property agents across the UK and, alongside Propertymark Qualifications, a provider of estate agency training and qualifications. He told me that political co-ordination of the regulation is complicated by the fact that the UK property market isn't just one market, and elements of housing law and property taxation are devolved to Scotland and Wales. It is made up of lots of different sub-markets, defined geographically, by building type and by activity. He says that, rightly, there is a government drive towards consumer protection and that, currently, there are just too many variables involved. We can assume then, that eventually the industry will be better regulated through licensed and qualified agents, but it hasn't yet received the green light from policy makers, and the lack of licensing and specific qualifications doesn't mean estate agents are completely untrained and unqualified. There are three main qualifying bodies of estate agents in the UK, of which Propertymark is the longest established. Propertymark has approximately 17,500 members and registered around 4,000 new candidates for exams in 2022.[8] The Guild of Property Professionals and Rightmove also provide training courses.

There is a focus in UK estate agency training on elements of the business such as law, compliance and negotiation of offers. There is relatively little emphasis on how to make a house look like something someone might want to buy. That's where you can step in to help your agent get you a great sale.

The legal bit

At this point, you may be worrying that you are about to trust the biggest financial transaction of your life, the sale of your house, to someone who is unqualified and unregulated. Let's have a look at the reality of this, the implications and the checks you can do to protect your own best interests.

The transaction process of selling a house *is* regulated. While it is true that estate agents are not licensed and do not need to be qualified,[9] they do need to act in accordance with the Estate Agents Act (1979)[10] and the Consumer Protection from Unfair Trading Regulations 2008.[11] The Estate Agents Act is a significant piece of legislation in the United Kingdom that regulates the activities of estate agents to ensure transparency, honesty and professionalism in the property market. As of October 2008, all residential estate agents in the UK must belong to an approved redress scheme, according to the Consumers, Estate Agents and Redress Act 2007.[12]

Estate agents are legally required to carry out identity and anti-money laundering checks on their clients, and there are hefty penalties for any agents that don't do these according to the guidelines and keep proper records. Agents are also required to abide by the Data Protection Act 2018.[13] You can be confident that your agent will protect the personal information they need to hold about you.

The National Trading Standards website has a property agent checker if you are in any doubt as to whether the agent you are planning to use is a legitimate business.

The human experience

According to Zoopla, the average length of time to sell a house in England is currently twenty-five weeks.[14] The average time it takes to get an offer, as I write, is 78 days.[15] Then add the time it takes from instructing your estate agent to bringing a house to the market – another two weeks – and you'll understand that you are in this for the long haul. Already, you are looking at almost eight months until you move, and that's if it all goes perfectly to plan.

You not only need a competent, trustworthy estate agent, you need one you like. You're going to talk to them a lot, over a long time. If you instruct an agent quickly in a rush to get on the market, you could find yourself having to change agents part-way through the process. This will only prolong things and lead to frustration on all sides. You may be going through other major life events that have triggered the need to sell. Divorce, bereavement, relocation for work – these are all stressful in themselves. Your estate agent will be walking alongside you on this emotional journey for the next few months; this being someone you trust from the outset is well worth the investment of time and energy it will take to find that person. Russell Quirk told me:

> 'Chemistry between you as the consumer and the agent is very important. If you don't like them, it doesn't really matter what they say about valuation or fee or what they've done locally, you won't want to use them.'

When you have found them, you need to listen to their advice. The biggest complaint I hear from agents about sellers is, 'I told them that at the start but they thought they knew better. Now we're having to reduce the price to what I suggested on day one.'

Conversely, the biggest complaint I hear from sellers about agents is, 'They told me my house was worth [high value]. Three weeks later they are telling me it isn't worth that at all and we have to reduce the price.'

It is an uncomfortable transition to the point where a much-loved home becomes the financial gateway to a new life stage. Agent and seller have to trust one another and communicate honestly to achieve the best results.

Summary

- Rightmove is the largest online property portal for the UK, hosting details of over one million homes at any one time.

- Post-pandemic buyers expect to see more information about a property online before scheduling a viewing.

- Sellers can choose between corporate, franchise, self-employed, independent, hybrid and online agent models. Their choice will determine the level of service and tools offered.

- The lack of licensing for estate agents in the UK is a factor contributing to the variable standards of agency practice. It is a legal requirement for all estate agents to adhere to the Estate Agent Act 1979 and the Consumer Protection from Unfair Trading Regulations 2008.

- All Propertymark member agents are not only professionally qualified, but also heavily regulated to above industry standards. Looking for an agent carrying the Propertymark protected logo is a good way to be sure you are working with a qualified professional.

- All estate agents must belong to an approved redress scheme, conduct identity and anti-money laundering checks and comply with data protection laws.

- Don't forget the human factor when choosing your estate agent. The process of selling your house will be long; you want to find someone you can trust.

2
Why Is A Marketing Strategy Important?

This chapter explains why you need an estate agent who will create a marketing strategy for your house, not one who will simply put it on Rightmove and pray. You'll learn:

- The difference between selling and marketing

- How to reach the 'zero moment of truth'

- About the 3Ps of property marketing – price, presentation and promotion

- How to recognise a good agent

What is a marketing strategy?

Seth Godin, a highly regarded marketing guru and author of many books on the subject, says that marketing is about making the ordinary remarkable.[16] Your home is your biggest financial asset. In a sea of ordinary homes on the internet, you need to make sure yours is remarkable.

To understand the difference between marketing a house and selling a house, let's take a quick look at how Philip Kotler, regarded as the father of modern marketing, distinguished between the two. Kotler describes marketing as the 'strategic, customer-centric process of identifying, creating, communicating, and delivering value to customers.'[17] In his view, marketing involves understanding customer needs, creating products or services that meet those needs and building long-term relationships. Sales on the other hand, according to Kotler, are tactical and transactional, with a process focused on converting leads into customers and achieving short-term revenue goals. He emphasises that 'unlike selling, marketing is fundamentally about understanding customers in order to develop products and services that meet needs.'

Seth Godin explains: 'Marketing tells a story that spreads. Sales overcomes the natural resistance to say yes.'[18] When you sell your home, you need both a marketing strategy, to attract buyers, and a salesperson who can close the deal on your behalf.

I asked Simon Leadbetter, ex-Countrywide, Knight Frank, Fine & Country and now Unchained, a marketing consultancy, how he sees the distinction between sales and marketing. He said:

'Where the industry gets really confused is they use the word "marketing" when they mean sales promotion. And promoting is probably only about 10% of what marketing is really about. If you look at the data from Rightmove and Twenty CI, people think about moving house for anything between three and seven years before they actually move. For instance, if they have a child then they might know that they need to move before the child reaches a certain age to get into a particular school. They've already thought about that. And that thought is going to be on their mind for a number of years before they start actively looking for a new home in the right area. Many life events happen with a year or two of advance knowledge of them. And that's where marketing comes in; it is the art of attracting the people who aren't yet in the market, to start seriously looking.'

This means that your buyer could be scrolling on Rightmove thinking that they will move in a year or two. If your house jumps out at them as being their dream home, they may decide to accelerate their plans. With great marketing, you can convert a dormant buyer into an active one.

The zero moment of truth

Jim Lecinski, then the marketing director of US Sales at Google, wrote *ZMOT: Winning the zero moment of truth* based on research he did at Google about how purchasing decisions are made.[19] The 'zero moment of truth' (ZMOT) describes a key moment in a purchasing decision.

What leads up to the ZMOT is important. Think about how you buy something. These days, we almost never buy on impulse; there is so much information available. Often, when you are looking to buy something, either a service or a product, you will go online first. When choosing your estate agent, you may get a recommendation from a friend. You will check out the agent's website. You might scroll through the properties they are selling on Rightmove or one of the other portals. You may follow their social media accounts or even ask a question of your own followers, 'Who do you think is the best agent to sell my house? Does anyone have any recommendations?' By the time you invite one or more agents to your home you will probably feel as though you already know them. You have effectively done the paper sift for a job interview they didn't even know they were applying for.

It is exactly the same for your buyer. By the time they book a viewing to see your home in real life for the first time, they will have done their research. Part of your role as a seller is to work with your estate agent to ensure that the content they need to complete this research is available and of a high enough quality for them to reach their ZMOT.

Lecinski's research says that to reach the ZMOT, you need to follow the 7–11–4 rule. On average, consumers spend seven hours researching a product, engage with eleven touchpoints, and do so in four different locations before deciding to buy. We can apply the 7–11–4 rule to the process of persuading someone to book a viewing of your house for sale. Let's look at the rule in more detail with that aim in mind.

7 hours of content

Seven hours of content will need to be available. This content will include the listing of your house, the photos and the videos your agent creates, though it would be unusual for your listing to contain seven hours of content by itself. Your buyer will also be looking for further, more diverse content to confirm that what they are buying is right for them. This might be a blog article about living in the area, information about local schools or connectivity to the nearest towns. It could be wider video content. Perhaps your agent's website has an introductory video about the neighbourhood or a podcast interviewing local businesses and residents about the benefits of living in the area. This type of content is important because it will help someone build a complete picture of whether this is somewhere they might like to live.

11 touch points

The touchpoints in a house-purchasing decision are the interactions between the agent and the potential buyer. While these will include all online interactions, such as visiting the agent's website, the property portals, social media posts and emails, they will also include the direct interactions the buyer has with the agent or the agent's office. Important touchpoints to consider before you engage an agent include: Who answers the phone when someone calls to book a viewing? Are they knowledgeable about your house? Can viewings be arranged at the convenience of the viewer, or only at the agent's convenience? I'm sure I'm not the only person who has decided not to buy a house because I simply can't get the agent, or seller, to arrange a viewing for a time when I'm not at work. It is unlikely that a buyer will be keen to make an offer if they believe, based on their early interactions with your agent, that they don't answer the phone or reply to voicemails promptly. This doesn't bode well for the progression phase of the purchase, where there are far more variables.

4 different locations

Your agent should be able to tell you where buyers are going in their hunt for information. Making sure relevant content about your house is readily available in these places is essential. Three of these locations will be the agent's website, the property portals and social media channels. The fourth might be the conversations with the agent and other staff members, and even print advertising or PR articles.

You will see by now that there is nothing in the research on how people decide to buy a high-value product that says, 'put poor-quality content on one online site and hope for the best.'

The 3Ps

There are three main elements to marketing a house: price, presentation and promotion. Once the sale has been agreed, the fourth P, progression, is what your agent will do. Choose your agent wisely and you will be in safe hands.

You will notice that many agents use the market appraisal, which is perhaps the first time you have met them, to tell you how big a market share they have in the local area. They give you a price at which they are prepared to list your home for sale and tell you what their fee will be. Often, you will only need to say, 'Oh, that's disappointing, agent one gave me a valuation of £20,000 more than that and their fee is 0.5% less than yours,' to trigger an about-turn and agent two will suddenly match agent one. This is a bad sign. Do not, under any circumstances, list with this agent.

Why not? Imagine that your buyer makes an offer of £20,000 less than the guide price on your home. Does this agent, who immediately backed down from their initial offer, seem like a fighter? Will they be standing up for a better offer on your behalf? The evidence says not. Find someone who can justify their valuation and knows their own worth in terms of the fee. That will be the agent who will fight for you at the negotiation stage with the buyer.

The other red flag is the agent who says, 'your house looks amazing, you don't need to do anything, we'll get it on the market by the weekend.' Call b***s*** on this agent too. About 1% of people live in a home that would look like a hugely desirable product with no work required. The other 99% of us simply can't live like this, because we have families. Partners, children, dogs. We have a life; we work from home, have friends over at the weekend and have too much stuff for our cupboards. The mantra of the best agents is, 'Speed to market does not equate to speed to sale.'

In other words, just because you list quickly, it doesn't mean you will find your buyer quickly. Time invested in ensuring your house is launched to the market with good preparation and a proper marketing strategy in place will never be wasted. The diagram below explains why it is so important to get all three Ps right from the outset.

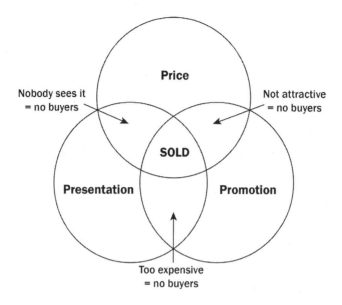

Let's take a brief look at each of the 3Ps now, though they will be covered in more detail in later chapters.

Price

Getting the price of your home right is the first thing your agent needs to do. You will probably invite three, even four agents to give you a valuation when you decide to sell. These valuations may vary quite a lot. It can be tempting to choose the agent who is offering to sell your home for the most money with the lowest fee. Have a think about that for a minute. In what other areas of your life do you get the best service for a low price?

What you are looking for is an agent who is prepared to spend time with you, who will give good advice and can support the valuation they give you with other similar, local examples. This kind of service and agent will inevitably come at a higher cost than the agent who rushes in and out without sharing any in-depth research or local comparisons. Time is money. The higher the fee, the more likely the agent is to allocate time to finding you a buyer and progressing your sale once you have accepted an offer. The extra 0.5% or even 1% you spend will pay dividends. And, of course, as a client paying for more, you can ask for more.

Russell Quirk worked as an estate agent for many years before moving into PR. He told me that there are a few 'catastrophic' ways to choose an agent:

> 'Never choose the highest valuation. Never choose the lowest fee and never choose an agent because they have the most "for sale" boards locally. What you should be looking for is an agent who is good at what they do.'

Pricing a property properly is an art, not an exact science. While there is a structure around valuation there is also a lot of market variation that comes into play. Unless your home is a standard kind of home on an estate where all the homes are similar in style, then deciding the price you should list it for is tricky. Jump to Chapter 4 for lots more detail on how to work with your estate agent to make sure your home is priced to achieve a great sale.

Presentation

Presentation is where things start to get a bit sketchy. Most estate agents aren't trained in helping you to present your home to market looking its best. The courses simply don't cover it. Lots of them know it's important and will give you great advice, but that advice tends to be fairly generic – declutter, paint the walls in a neutral colour, tidy the garden etc. Lots of agents won't tell you what you need to do about the presentation of your home to appeal to your target buyer even if you ask. They are scared that you will be upset if they mention that most buyers looking for a home like yours will be put off by your dated décor and the fact that the house smells of dogs. Many will let you list it as it is, leaving it up to you what you want people to see. Do not list your home without following the advice I provide in the presentation chapter. It may sell, but you certainly won't get the best price for it.

Your agent may be scared that if you take time to prepare the house properly for sale then you might change your mind about listing with them, or even selling at all. The way to identify an estate agent with this mindset is to ask them to recommend a home-staging business. If they have a preferred partner for getting the presentation right, they will be confident they are not going to lose your business. They will be bringing in experts to help you and you will be coming to market ready to achieve the best sale possible. It doesn't have to cost you anything. Many staging businesses, including mine, will give advice for free. Chapter 5 deals with presentation in more detail and my first book covers the topic extensively, with lots of tips and tricks for the DIY stager.

Once the presentation has been done you must make sure you get great photos. Irrespective of your price point in the market, professional photography is essential. It is worth the cost. Just look on the portals for a few minutes to understand that almost every estate agent who says, 'I've got a good camera, I'll do your photos,' is deluded about their abilities as a photographer.

Promotion

Promotion is what your agent does with your listing once it is ready to launch. Are they planning to put the details on Rightmove, make themselves a coffee and wait for the phone to ring? Or will the house be talked about on their social media platforms, both before launch and once it is fully ready? Will they be going through their database of prospective buyers and making calls? You are paying the bill; ask these questions before you agree the fee.

Online marketing via the property portals and social media is critically important. If you look at any of the property listings in the United States, especially at the higher end of the market, the lifestyle videos are amazing. They sell every aspect of living in a home. They don't stop to explain, 'There is a kitchen with an oven and an extractor over the hob' in the way that many UK listings do. They create videos that show people living in the home, having fun cooking for their friends and eating outdoors on the patio with their family. Why would you not buy a house marketed like this? From the screen, it already looks and feels like a fabulous place to live. We haven't yet reached the stage where this is the norm in the UK. It will come.

In the last few years, UK estate agents have begun to realise that their social media channels are a great way to reach a buyer directly. Far more people have grown up buying everything they need online, often after seeing a video on TikTok or a reel on Instagram. We suggest that our clients ask their agent to do a 'coming soon' video clip. This is like the trailer for a new film that's being released; it shows some of the best bits, just enough to make a potential buyer think, 'I need to call the agent and make sure I am the first to view that house.' You want the purchase of your house to become a competition, to turn into a bidding war because so many people are interested.

Signs of a good agent

We work with a lot of agents nationwide. There is a big difference in the kinds of answers you will get when you ask them to 'tell me about the marketing strategy for my home.' Some will have no clue what you are asking. They will tell you that they'll be round on Saturday to take some photos and then it'll go on Rightmove. Throw that agent out of your house now. They won't get you the best sale. I don't care if they're the cheapest – get them out.

Great marketing is not a club reserved for expensive houses; your house is the financial gateway to your future regardless of whether it is a two-bed terrace in Leeds or a ten-bed mansion in Surrey. What will a good agent talk about when you ask about a marketing strategy? At every price point you can expect an agent to discuss:

- A valuation support by current, comparable evidence

- A pricing strategy that acknowledges the difference in launch strategy depending on whether you use a higher, medium or lower valuation

- Advice about the target buyer for your home

- Advice about how best to present your home

- A viewing strategy

- Listing your home on their website and the big property portals

- Professional photography

- A video tour

- Promotion of your house on social media

If you are selling a home at the premium end of the market, they may also offer you:

- The option of a discreet listing

- Listing on international portals

- A high-quality printed brochure

- PR or advertising in a national publication

- The opportunity to include an interview with you on the listing

Contract length

A word about contract length. Some agents still try to tie their sellers into lengthy agreements. Be wary of this. John Durrant, marketing guru and industry expert, says, 'The only credible reason for a sole agency lasting half a year is the agent's lack of confidence in finding a buyer quickly.'[20]

While your agent may not be looking to sign you up for as much as twenty-six weeks, many still want a twelve-week contract. Think about whether this is in your best interests before you sign. You need to be confident that your chosen agent will absolutely be doing their best for you on all fronts – price, presentation and promotion. Three months is a long time. Many agents now work on a 'no fixed term' contract where, if you're not happy, you can change agents at any time.

Your role as the seller is to listen and take advice. You will have done your research before inviting an agent to your home. Now is the time to listen to what they have to say and to take the advice they offer. Remember, the biggest mistake you can make as a seller is to instruct the agent who will list your home at the highest price while offering the cheapest fee. These are the sellers who, in Durrant's words, 'still believe in Santa Claus and are blinded by the promise of an unrealistic price, so much so that they don't bother reading or questioning their agent's terms.'[21] Don't let this be you.

Summary

- Find an estate agent you trust and who prioritises creating a robust marketing strategy over simply listing the property, and be willing to listen to their advice. Choose an agent based on good advice and a valuation supported by local examples and resist the temptation to opt for the highest valuation and lowest fee.

- The 3Ps of property marketing are: price, presentation and promotion.

- There is a difference between marketing and selling. Effective marketing is about creating a great listing and attracting potential buyers.

- Buyers often plan a move years in advance, making it important to use marketing to attract those not actively looking.

- The zero moment of truth is a significant part of a purchasing decision and highlights the need to have high-quality content in the right places.

- Collaborate with your chosen estate agent (and potentially a home-staging expert) to present your home in a way that will appeal to your target buyer.

- Discuss with your agent how the property will be promoted, including professional photography, compelling videos and active use of digital and print marketing channels.

3
The Preparation Phase

By the end of this chapter, you will be exhausted. But you will understand:

- The importance of getting yourself and your family mentally prepared for a move

- How to objectively assess what you need to do to get your house ready to achieve the best sale possible

- The financial and emotional cost of not preparing properly

Moving house is one of life's most stressful events, along with death and divorce, both of which are common companions on a house-moving journey. Taking time to prepare, to look ahead and to understand what your stress triggers might be, will pay dividends in managing your move.

Why is the preparation phase so important? Iain Kennedy, who was the chief marketing officer for Rightmove for eight years, pointed out to me that not all property listings are the same – there is a noticeable variation in quality. Some capture the imagination much more than others. You want yours to be the one that grabs buyers' attention, and that doesn't happen overnight. Preparation is key.

Preparing yourself

We prepare meticulously for lots of relatively minor events in our lives. When we have a job interview, we spend time researching the company; we ask questions of other people who may know someone who works there; we buy a new outfit. For big events, such as a wedding or holiday, or even buying a new car, the research and preparation can take months. It fascinates me that we can be so careful in these preparations, and yet we meet lots of sellers who have decided to sell their house and called the local agent thinking that's all that they need to do.

The process of buying and selling a home in England is lengthy, complicated and sometimes unfair. The first step is to understand this and accept that that's how it is right now. Against this backdrop, some specific things you need to be prepared for are:

- Finding an estate agent and solicitor you trust

- Agreeing a marketing plan

- Preparing your home for a succession of people, all of whom will be looking with a critical eye at how you live

- Living in a tidy house, or endlessly tidying, before viewings

- Not getting any viewings

- Negotiating and re-negotiating the price

- Agreeing an offer one day only to have the buyer pull out the next

- Progressing your sale to the day before exchange (in itself a feat of chasing the agent, solicitor, buyer and the buyer's cat, all of whom will tell you a completely different story about the same set of events), only to have your buyer pull out giving no reason at all

- Getting the sale to exchange and then actually having to pack and move house

- Persuading your kids, partner and the dog that moving is going to happen on Tuesday whether they like it or not

- Buying another house that everyone likes (except you, because your opinion has become largely irrelevant, you just chase paperwork, emails and phone calls)

- Progressing your purchase to exchange (all of the above apply again), only to have your seller pull out the day before exchange, giving no reason at all

To help you do all this, you need a team you can trust to help move things forward even when it's all going horribly wrong. Make sure your whole family are on side with the move, both with selling your current home and choosing the new one. Talk about it often and at length, and agree what's OK and what's not before you start. Gather your friends and ask for their unfailing support, sympathy and patience for the next few months – and for their practical help in making your home look amazing. Make sure you build in treats, or time out for you, every week. Plan things to look forward to that will keep you going through exciting changes and challenging moments.

Preparing your home

Once you feel prepared for the mental challenge of moving home, the next step is the physical challenge of preparing your home for a stream of visitors. Here, you need a critical eye. All your viewers will be looking for reasons to pay less for your home than you are asking for it. I liken it to taking a car to WeBuyAnyCar. com. Online, the price you get once you've put in your details is good. On the forecourt, though, the assessor comes out and finds scratches you have completely forgotten about and rotting banana skins under the kids' seats that finally explain the smell that's been puzzling you. By the time the assessor has finished finding flaws, you feel grateful that they will take the car off your hands at all.

Prepare and pre-empt the equivalent situation with your home. Start by approaching your home from the outside, as a prospective buyer will. Walk, or drive, down the road. Can you find the address easily? Is the house number or name visible to someone who has no idea where you are?

Then, walk around with a camera. Take lots of photos from every single angle in every single room. Once you have a full set of photos, load them onto a big screen, don't view them on your phone. Use a laptop or, even better, a TV screen. You will notice things about the house you hadn't ever thought about – clutter lurking in corners, marks on walls and stains on the carpets. These are all normal parts of living in a home, but they are also things your buyers will notice and turn their noses up at. Clutter, scuffs and stains are not Instagram-worthy. When a potential buyer has viewed your home, they may want to post photos on their social media channels to gauge the opinion of their friends and family.

My advice would be to allow a month for every year you have lived in a house to get it ready for a sale, if you can. In some cases – divorce, bereavement, suddenly finding your dream home – this just isn't possible. But if you can allow the time, the whole process will be less stressful. Both you and the house will come to market fully prepared. If you don't have that amount of time, consider enlisting professional help.

The detailed steps you can take to make your home look its absolute best are in Chapter 5 – come to that chapter armed with your photos.

Kerb appeal

You will no doubt have seen articles and advice about the importance of kerb appeal. But what does it even mean? Kerb appeal is the look of the house from the outside – traditionally from the kerb, but these days it applies even to the photos on the property portals. Kerb appeal is what makes someone stop and take notice of your house.

You have every opportunity to increase your kerb appeal before you sell. In terms of the physical kerb appeal, this means getting the DIY jobs done. Repair window frames, rehang the gate and move the dustbins. Tidy the garden, paint the front door and mow the lawn.

When thinking about virtual kerb appeal, you want your photos to be as attractive as possible. Make sure that everything your online viewers see is striking enough that they will want to stop and see more. The photos should encourage them to call the estate agent and book a viewing. Swiping right on Rightmove is the virtual equivalent of having done a drive-by and not wanting to see inside after all.

Your potential viewers may well do both a virtual and physical drive-by before they book a viewing. Both will contribute to the 7–11–4 rule when it comes to the decision to view. You are in control of the first impression viewers have.

Take note of current trends

What else are your buyers seeing in your photos? They will be able to tell your taste in décor and how recently you have decorated your home, both inside and out. Interior design is a fashion-led industry. Fortunately, the macro trends don't seem to change as often as they do in clothing, but many people are put off viewing a home that looks dated or the colour palette isn't to their taste.

Some sellers don't see the point of decorating if they are going to move anyway. Culturally, we have an expectation that a buyer is going to 'do work' to the house after they buy it and so there is no point making changes ahead of selling. This has changed dramatically in the last twenty years with the advent of online property portals and societal shifts. The ratio of house prices and mortgages to earnings is very different to forty years ago. Buyers today typically have less disposable income and less time to spend on DIY in their new home. The turnkey property is the one that attracts most interest and, therefore, the highest offers.

Taking time to research current home trends before you sell will pay dividends. Much of the advice will tell you to 'paint the walls a neutral colour.' Be careful, though, one neutral is not the same as another. Colours can be warm or cold and getting it wrong, even with a neutral, will significantly impact how a house feels when visitors walk through the door.

CASE STUDY: Right house, wrong grey

Years ago, we were involved with a three-bedroom home in a nice village close to our office. The family had relocated for work and taken all their furniture with them. Before they left, they redecorated the whole house in a fashionable grey. The house was still on the market four months later and there was little interest in it, so we were called in to see if we could shed some light on what the problem might be.

The colour in itself was beautiful and in many houses would have been the perfect solution. In this house, though, the source of natural light in the main rooms came from the north. The grey looked depressing because the light was so poor. And as there was no furniture, there was nothing to showcase the lifestyle the property offered. Our first step was to paint the walls a soft off-white from a cream palette, not grey. Then we furnished the house. A week or so later, the estate agent told me she'd practically had to move into the house, given how many viewings she was doing. An offer was accepted within two weeks of the changes being made.

While it makes sense that you wouldn't want to completely renovate your home based on the latest interiors craze, it is easy to make small additions that acknowledge trends without breaking the bank. For example, an interiors trend that has been significant over the last year or two is natural textures and home crafts; changing fabric lampshades for ones made of rattan or adding a few woven cushions is an easy and cheap way to incorporate this. These small changes may be the trigger that attracts someone to book a viewing. Acknowledging trends can give the subliminal message that, as a seller, you are on the ball and will be moving the sale forward quickly. Simple changes can make a huge difference to the number of viewings that are booked.

DIY

When you walk through your home taking photos in the preparation stage of your sale, you will probably notice jobs that need to be done. We all walk past scuffs in the hallway. My son's bike is much too precious to live outside. If he's home, there are always scuffs at handlebar height. Maybe the hinges on the kitchen cupboards have dropped slightly so the doors don't quite close, or the grout in the shower is mouldy in one corner. You will usually overlook these details because they're not important in daily life. Your buyer won't overlook them. And once they notice one job they think needs to be done, they will notice all the others. That may well result in your property being placed on their 'no' list because it 'needs too much work.'

The 'work' they are predicting may in reality be a weekend of DIY, nothing serious at all. Their choice to move on and look at more houses because they are not in love with yours will be deeply frustrating for you. There's a solution – do all the little jobs yourself before any viewers arrive. It is even worth the investment to get professional help. A couple of days paying a plumber, a decorator or a gardener is a tiny outlay compared to months of not selling your home and then being forced to accept a low offer.

A well-maintained home sends the message: 'We care about our home, and we care about the person who wants to buy it enough to make the sale progress quickly and smoothly.'

CASE STUDY: A quick £60k

I was asked to visit the new home of a client, Frances, who we had worked for earlier in the year. When we first met, Frances was struggling. Her home had been listed for more than £800,000 and failed to attract any significant interest; it sat on the market for a while and she had eventually accepted an offer at £750,000. She wanted to move on and so had accepted a low offer. Luckily, as it turned out, the sale fell through.

The new agent asked us to get involved and we worked with Frances using her furniture and accessories, with a few additions from our stock, to make the house look more appealing. Crucially, we did a few minor repairs, those irritating niggly ones you stop noticing when you live in a house but every buyer believes mean 'work'. We had the front door repainted in a gorgeous blue and changed a cracked shower tray. We replaced a door that had been broken and no-one had bothered to repair because it wasn't often used. Within a few weeks, Frances had accepted an offer of £820,000.

When I reunited with Frances to help with some interior design for her new home, she told me: 'All my friends thought it was ridiculous to spend money on a home I was moving out of. They thought that getting it staged was a mad idea and a lot of unnecessary expense. They're not laughing at me now. I'm over £60,000 better off than I would have been if the original sale had completed, even taking the higher agent fees and the staging costs into account.'

Good preparation for your sale isn't about cost, it's about investment. It is what ensures that the sale actually happens, and more than pays for itself in the process.

Do your sums

How much does it cost to run your home per month? If you don't know, or your estimate is a bit out of date because bills have changed, then now is the time to work it out in detail. Include the mortgage payments, council tax, utility bills and any other standing payments that are essential for the upkeep. Every month your home is on the market without attracting a sale, this is money that you're wasting. What's more, the longer your home sits on the market without finding a buyer, the lower the price you will eventually sell for. It's a double whammy. There are some scary stats about the real cost of a price drop in Chapter 4. For now, know that it is essential that your home is launched to market well-prepared and primed to attract your target buyer – and quickly.

CASE STUDY: Cheering up a sad house

One home in our portfolio that stands out for me is a fabulous farmhouse in the Leicestershire countryside. When I first saw it, it had been on the market for about seven months, with little interest and no acceptable offers. The main part of the house had been built in the 1700s and it had a '60s style extension. The older part was beautiful externally but, like many old houses, felt slightly damp and neglected inside. The owners were divorcing, one partner had left already, taking much of the furniture. You begin to get the picture of a sad house.

The agent who asked us to take a look understood the value we could bring by adding more furniture and generally creating a lived-in feel to the house. Within a week of having added furniture, artwork and lots of soft furnishings and accessories, the house had not only been relaunched with a new set of photos, but the owners had accepted an offer 7% over the original asking price. At a guide price of £1million and with a staging cost of about £10,000, this meant that the sellers were £110,000 better off than they would have been if they had decided to stay with the agent they'd first instructed, who could only suggest they drop the price to £950,000 to try to get a sale.

Summary

- It is important to prepare yourself (and your family members), mentally, physically and emotionally, for the stress of moving, which is amongst life's most challenging events. The entire family must be (and stay) on board with the decision to sell and lines of communication should be open to address concerns and expectations.

- You need to objectively assess and prepare your home for the best possible sale, and understand the financial and emotional costs of inadequate preparation. Seek professional help if you don't have the time, energy or inclination to do it yourself.

- Be prepared for unexpected events, including negotiations and buyers pulling out, and be flexible in dealing with setbacks throughout the selling journey.

- Visual appeal, both in person and online, is hugely important. There are many strategies to achieve this – taking quality photos, enhancing kerb appeal and keeping up with interior design trends. Small changes can make a big difference. Make sure your home is appealing from the outside, both in the photos and when a viewer arrives.

- Address minor repairs and outstanding DIY jobs to present a well-maintained home, which is more appealing to potential buyers.

- There are monthly costs associated with maintaining your home while it's on the market, and a prolonged selling period will have a financial impact. This underscores the importance of a well-prepared launch.

- Preparation is an investment rather than a cost, as it facilitates a smoother selling process and will often result in a significantly higher final sale price and a quicker sale.

4
Price And Fees

B y the time you get to the end of this chapter you will:

- Have an idea of how an estate agent reaches their valuation

- Understand why getting your pricing strategy right from the outset is the quickest route to maximising your sale

- Know how much you should be paying your estate agent and what you can expect to get for their fee

Price really is the million-dollar question. It is easy to be seduced into listing with the agent who values your home the highest and promises you the lowest fees. Why wouldn't you? In *Sell High, Sell Fast*, I wrote:

> 'A product will be bought at its highest price quickly, if it's desirable. Any product which is less desirable will take longer to sell and will eventually be bought at a lower price point. This has been evident in the property market for many years. The longer a property remains on the market with no buyer, the more the price will be decreased to try to attract interest. The properties which are snapped up quickly tend to be sold at, or even over, their original guide price.'

The statistical data cited in the section of this chapter on price reductions is evidence of the truth of this statement.

How does an estate agent price a house?

How the guide price of a house is reached is a complex process. There are many factors influencing the final figure and, in the end, like any other product, the price it sells for is whatever the buyer is willing to pay for it.

The Royal Institute of Chartered Surveyors (RICS) teaches property valuation based on the condition of the property, its location, market trends and sales data from similar properties.[22] There will be significant regional variations and even local variation in the average price per square foot of a home. Chartered surveyors tend to do mortgage valuations for the lenders, matrimonial valuations for court cases in a divorce and insurance valuations. But it's your estate agent, who won't have gone through as rigorous of a valuation training process as a chartered surveyor does, who is the go-to person for your market appraisal ahead of a sale.

Your estate agent will be able to advise of the range of prices that are being achieved locally for homes like yours. You can expect them to bring comparable evidence to the market appraisal, or even send it ahead, to discuss with you to decide what your guide price should be. Whether they are prepared to list it at the top of that range or at the bottom will depend on how well the house has been maintained and on how it is presented. This is a good reason to do any repairs before your estate agent arrives and perhaps even think about the presentation before you invite them over. We start working with a lot of sellers before they have instructed an agent, to make sure the guide price they are quoted is the best it can be.

The pricing strategy

Once the valuation range has been determined, based on the factors mentioned above, it is time to think tactically. This means deciding on the best pricing strategy, as part of the wider marketing strategy, for your launch to market.

Three prices should be discussed at the market appraisal. The first is the aspirational price that someone will pay if they see yours as their dream home. This is usually about 10% over the average market value. The US-based National Association of Realtors research says that at 10% over market price, about 30% of your potential buyers will notice your listing.[23] This may be the price your agent suggests you start with if you plan to launch as a discreet listing. It will also be the 'coming soon' price that your agent should be pitching to their database of hot buyers – more about this in Chapter 9.

The second price is the realistic market price, the one at which at least 60% of your potential buyers will notice your home. The third is the one that may be used by your agent as the 'offers over' price. This will be about 10% lower than the price they anticipate being able to achieve for you.[24] The psychology behind using the lower price is to draw in a wider audience, around 75% of people who may be looking for a home like yours. The intention is to generate more competition and so push the offers up to and even beyond, the middle pricing bracket.

At this stage, you and your agent should be discussing the price for your home in conjunction with the strategy they will use when they launch your listing.

You may find that the 'high valuation, low fee' agents think nothing of listing your home on the portals at the aspirational price on day one. 'We'll go high – we can always come down.' 'People will look and offer lower anyway so we might as well launch high.' You may also feel that this is a good tactic.

This is not a strategic approach; it's gambling with your financial future. Whether the launch price was set by you or your agent, your agent will come to you a couple of weeks later and say that 'the lack of interest is telling us that your house is too expensive.' No, it wasn't too expensive; launching on Rightmove at the aspirational price was a poor strategy. The aspirational price is only achievable if there are 'hot' buyers who will view and make an offer before the listing goes live. The following figure is well-used in the industry and perfectly illustrates the issue of pricing too high.

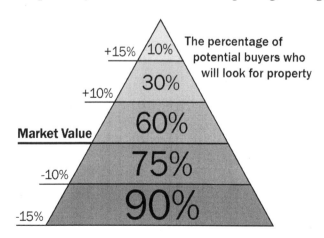

Impact of price on visibility

When your house is launched to Rightmove you should be deciding between the realistic and the slightly lower 'offers over' price. The decision about which you use isn't isolated; it will be governed by the overall marketing strategy. As a client, you need to clearly understand your role in influencing the pricing strategy; if you insist on listing at the aspirational price, as some agents tell me their clients do, then you shouldn't be surprised or disappointed when the price has to drop in a few weeks. You will have played a part in the failure to attract the right buyer.

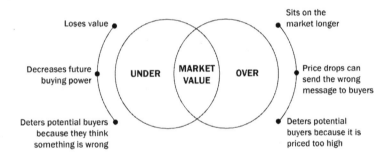

Pricing your home[25]

Why correct pricing matters

If your home is priced correctly for the market at the time you sell, there will be a number of positive impacts. Note that I say, 'at the time you sell.'

There is often a gap between a seller's perception of the market and a buyer's perception. In a falling market, the seller's view will be subject to a lag; in other words, they will still be optimistic about the price they can achieve. By contrast, from the buyer's view, they will be anticipating a bigger fall in the market than has actually happened and so will want to pay much less than the seller's still-optimistic expectation. The reverse will be true in a rising market: a seller will usually get too optimistic, too soon, with the result still being that the buyer is expecting to pay less than the seller imagines.

Correct pricing will attract several interested prospective buyers. The more people who are interested in your home, the more likely you are to sell. There will probably be other houses similar to yours on the market in the same area at the same time. If yours seems expensive against the competition then you won't attract viewings, much less offers. If it looks too cheap compared to the others it will immediately arouse suspicion – what's wrong with it? If you get the price right then you should have multiple interested parties and will achieve your guide price, or even higher, in a short time.

Don't leave the pricing strategy entirely up to your estate agent. You can research the competition before you meet with them. Remember that someone who is looking for a four-bedroom home in your area will also be looking in neighbouring towns or villages and may also be viewing properties in the price brackets above and below where you think yours should sit. They will want to see what else they could get for their money.

We come across sellers who bought their home when the market was buoyant and subsequently spent a considerable sum of money on renovations or interior design. They often believe that the way to price their home is to add up everything it has cost them, add a bit on top and that is the minimum amount they will accept. Trying to build profit into selling a house, unless you are a developer, doesn't work. How much a house is worth is driven by more complex factors than the money it has cost the current occupier. If the market is falling when you sell and you bought recently in a buoyant market, you may have negative equity in the house. A house being worth less than it has cost you is a hard thing to understand and accept if circumstance dictates that you have no choice about when you move. We see situations where the guide price of the house is a number the homeowner has insisted upon against the advice of their estate agent. This is highly damaging for the relationship, inevitably resulting in a loss of trust between agent and client when the house fails to attract offers that meet the unrealistic aspirations of the seller. Each will blame the other, a new agent is instructed and the cycle starts again. This is stressful for everyone involved and never results in a good sale. Choose your agent wisely and listen to their advice.

The scourge of the price reduction

If you are in the group of sellers who are still determined to believe it is better to list your home at the aspirational price because you are 'willing to take an offer' then this section is for you.

Research conducted over six years by Tim Bannister, director at Rightmove, shows that properties that have been reduced behave quite differently to those that don't go through a price reduction. For example, the SSTC rate for reduced compared to non-reduced listings from January 2017 to December 2022 indicates that the reduced properties are 10% less likely to be sold. Not 'sold at their guide price' but sold *at all*. That's a huge penalty for insisting on going to market with a hopeful asking price.

It gets worse. The same set of statistics tell us that properties that have been reduced take more than double the time of non-reduced homes to go under offer, and the seller is almost twice as likely to change agents.[26] Remember, every minute of extra time on the market is costing you money.

If you take nothing else away from this book, please take away this advice: it is *always* a bad idea to over-price your house when you launch to market. Find a good agent, listen to them, look at the comparable evidence they present and go with their advice.

Price brackets

When you are talking about the guide price for your home take note of the price brackets on the portals such as Rightmove, Zoopla and On The Market. Why is this important to consider?

When you are searching for your new home, first you put the area you are looking to move to into the search bar. Then you go to the filters and put in the number of bedrooms and the price bracket you are searching in, along with some other keywords. When you put in your maximum price you will have to choose from a dropdown list. Let's say your maximum is £500,000. When the results pop up, the first houses you see will have a price tag of £500,000. If this is your budget, then you will scroll through those houses first and perhaps pick a few to view.

If you are the seller and your house is priced at £495,000, someone looking with a £500,000 budget may see twenty houses at £500,000 before they even get to your listing. By the time they reach yours, it will probably be on their reserve list. Ask your agent to make sure your valuation is at the top of a price bracket so it comes up close to the top of a search for someone browsing. Don't let it get lost in the 'also ran' list.

A tale of two agents

Estate agent fees in the UK currently range between 0.5% + VAT and 2.5% + VAT of the guide price. On a £500,000 house, this is the difference between paying your agent £3,000 and £15,000. On the face of it, the £12,000 difference is a lot of money.

Scenario 1

Let's say that your agent with a fee of 0.5% tells you your home is worth £500,000 and lists it on Rightmove for exactly that. You sign a twelve-week contract with them and they get it onto the market quickly, having taken a range of photos on their iPhone. In the first two weeks, the so-called 'golden window', you have two viewings. You show both viewers around as your estate agent doesn't do accompanied viewings for 0.5%. You have to do a lot of tidying up both times and send the kids to the cinema with their grandparents, which costs you a fortune. Neither set of viewers is particularly interested. They arrived seemingly unaware that your house didn't have a separate room to be used as a study and both families needed a space to work from home sometimes. You told them they could make the fourth bedroom into a study, but they didn't want to make an offer. Once the twelve-week contract comes to an end you change agents. You agree to a higher fee of 1.2% with the new agent and accept an offer of £485,000. You end up with £477,800 after paying the agent £7,200 (£6,000 + VAT). Altogether, your sale took nine months to reach completion.

Scenario 2

Let's take the other extreme. You decide to go with the agent charging 2.5% because they come highly recommended by friends. It seems pretty extravagant but your friends achieved a great sale for their home six months ago. The good news is that this agent has no minimum term contract so at least if they don't find you a buyer quickly you can change agents with no notice. This agent arrives with lots of examples of homes they have successfully sold in your area recently. You're impressed so far. But they don't want you to get on the market straight away. Is that a red flag? They suggest that first you speak to their professional staging team – there is no charge for the consultation. The staging team recommend that you do lots of decluttering, with the idea being that you will then be ready for your move and the clearer rooms will photograph better. Seems like pretty sensible advice. They also tell you to take the bed out of the fourth bedroom and rent some furniture to make it look like a great home office. The cost of the rental and their help styling the house before the photographer arrives is £2000.

You have paid an upfront marketing fee to your agent, £1000 of which covers the costs of the professional photographer and a videographer. You're excited about this because you've seen the videos they produce and they're fabulous. While all this is going on, the estate agent creates a little teaser video to post on social media, which shows off the best bits of the house (the bits you've already tidied up). The video mentions the house is 'coming soon' and, by the time you have everything ready, two weeks have passed but several people are interested.

The agent's strategy to launch your home to market is to do three weeks of full marketing with the new photos and a longer video. These go out on the normal portals, including Rightmove, and on their social media channels. Your agent presents the video themselves, talking about the features of the house, with little clips of the seating area you love in the garden and the log fire lit for the winter months. The agent has even interviewed you and included a few quotes from you about what you have loved most about living here – a great chance to tell a new family about the park just up the road and your favourite coffee shop in town.

Then comes the open day. Just one day you need to tidy up for, with ten sets of prospective buyers arriving at various times. Thankfully, the agent is doing all the viewings and has suggested you go out for the day as a family.

Well, that was Saturday. Today, Monday, lots of people have phoned who love the house and want to make an offer. Your agent advises that the best buyer, although not the highest offer, is a family living locally in a rented house. They have had to relocate for work; they sold their home a few months ago, the kids are settling in at their new school and they need to find their new home in this town. Their offer is £530,000. Even after paying the estate agent and the staging costs, you will have realised £512,000 within four months including the time to completion.

Cheapest isn't always best. The next chapters will unpick each element of the marketing strategy to show how paying a higher fee will allow your estate agent to do far more on your behalf.

Summary

- Pricing is a crucial factor in selling a house, and it's important to get it right from the beginning.

- The process of pricing a house considers factors like property condition, location, market trends and sales data from similar properties.

- Estate agents play a role in determining the pricing strategy, suggesting aspirational, realistic and 'offers over' prices.

- The aspirational price is about 10% over market value, targeting potential buyers who see the property as their dream home.

- The realistic market price is set to attract at least 60% of potential buyers, while the 'offers over' price is used to generate competition.

- Launching at the aspirational price without a strategic approach is risky and will almost certainly lead to price reductions later.

- Price reductions are likely to mean your home takes twice as long to sell or may not sell at all.

- Sellers should research competition and understand the market to avoid overpricing based on, for example, renovation costs.

- The pricing strategy should consider price brackets on online portals to maximise the listing's visibility.

- Paying a higher estate agent fee will open up more comprehensive marketing strategies, leading to a quicker and more lucrative sale.

PART TWO
PRESENTATION

5
The Role Of Home Staging

I n the next few pages, you will learn:

- What home staging is and why it's important in maximising your sale

- The seven-step process to perfect presentation

- What you can do yourself to get the presentation right and when to call in a professional

Ten years ago, most estate agents and home sellers in the UK knew nothing about home staging. If they had heard of it, it was seen as an 'American fad' and certainly not a normal part of the house selling process. In my opinion, there is no point in launching a house to market without doing some staging first.

You can choose to do this yourself and I will tell you how and where to find the information you need to do it well. Or you can engage the services of a professional. I have included in this chapter some questions to ask a professional stager to ensure you get value for your money.

When multiple lockdowns meant that in-person viewings were difficult or impossible, estate agents had to get creative in the way they did viewings. Many turned to video, virtual tours, WhatsApp and Facebook viewings. Both agents and homeowners quickly realised that with this level of scrutiny, the presentation of the home had become super important. It's amazing how seeing our own home through the lens of a camera can help us spot things we would normally walk past without noticing.

The need for great photos and detailed videos hasn't gone away since people have been able to view homes in person again. There are many reasons why potential buyers will look extensively at photos and videos before they book a viewing. As a seller, this is good news. The more online tools someone is able to utilise to get a feel for your home, the fewer time wasters you will get in real life. Well-presented homes will attract more viewings and increase the amount of time a viewer spends in the home.[27] Good estate agents have carried the focus on nailing the presentation through into their post-pandemic marketing efforts.

What is home staging?

In essence, 'home staging' means 'preparing a home for sale'. The goal of staging is to make a home appealing to the highest number of potential buyers, helping it to sell more swiftly and for more money. Staging techniques focus on improving a property's appeal by transforming it into a welcoming, attractive product that more than one buyer will fall in love with. You're aiming to communicate the lifestyle your home offers to a new owner. Buying a home is a joint decision, involving both the head and the heart. Staging is the tool that will enable you to capture the heart; it will make viewers fall in love with your home and quickly put an offer on the table, one which is realistic and reflects the price your agent has suggested.

Until relatively recently, staging was not widely used in the UK property market. But in the last five years, the interest in staging a home before sale in the UK has doubled.[28] While this hasn't yet brought it to the levels seen in other parts of the world, especially the US and Australia, it does mean that presentation is considered in far more home sales than ever before.

When is staging useful?

Any estate agent that tells you your house is fine to list exactly as it is, is either deluded or desperate. Very few people live in a way which would allow their house to be launched to market without anything needing to be done. If you are amongst those few, you can skip this chapter. If not, read on.

Staging helps homeowners to sell their homes quicker and get better offers. The range of services offered by professional staging businesses in the UK varies from a simple consultation followed by a written report detailing how a homeowner can help themselves achieve the best sale, right through to fully furnishing an empty home.

Engaging the services of a professional stager can be helpful if, as a seller, you don't have the time, energy or vision to make the changes necessary to make your home more attractive to buyers. We work with families who have lived in their homes for many years and simply can't face the laborious process of sorting, organising and getting rid of unwanted belongings ahead of a move. We also work with professional people who just don't have time to think about their move. Many of our clients are working hard and don't want to spend weekends redecorating before they sell. We help couples divorcing, where a third-party opinion can help smooth out a difficult situation. We work with families who have been bereaved and can't face emptying the home of a loved one. Getting ready for a sale is hard work, but you don't have to do it alone.

DIY or hire a professional?

Staging, like any professional service, comes at a cost. As a seller, you may prefer to go it alone and stage the house yourself. This can be highly successful. There are many articles on how to do this and glossy magazines, the property press and staging businesses will all publish their top tips. I wrote the first book in the UK that explained to home sellers, in detail, exactly how to stage their home. If an estate agent has a good relationship with a local stager, they will usually offer an initial, probably verbal, consultation without charge. All of this resource is available to help you as a seller prepare your home for the best possible sale. Use it.

In the UK at the moment there are around a hundred staging businesses that are members of the only UK professional industry body, the Home Staging Association of the UK and Ireland. There are, of course, other businesses that don't belong to the professional association and also furniture rental businesses that now offer staging as part of their service. Every one of them sets out to help sellers increase the selling price of their home and to achieve a sale quickly.

I describe using professional staging as a bit like taking your car to the garage for a service. There are many online videos detailing how to service a car engine, so in theory you could do it yourself. But in the garage, they do it every day. They have the proper tools for the job and are far less likely to make a costly mistake. It is especially useful if you need to achieve a quick sale and don't have time to do the preparation needed yourself.

CASE STUDY: Operation tidy-up

We had a good example of staging facilitating a quick sale when we were asked to help with a home on the outskirts of Leicester. The owner, Annie, called and said, 'Elaine, we weren't intending to move but our dream home has just come up in the village we have loved forever. The owners of the house we want to buy are elderly and keen for a quick sale. We're not even on the market. We've spoken to them and they have agreed to give us one month to get a sale agreed on ours. If we can achieve that, they will accept the offer we have already submitted.'

Annie, her husband and their two teenage children had lived in their current home for about ten years. It was a great family home with open-plan living space and four big bedrooms. But Annie rightly recognised that they had two main challenges to overcome to achieve a quick offer at the kind of figure they needed to buy their dream house, which needed significant renovation. They needed an offer that gave them the spare cash they would need.

First, their home looked 'lived in'. You know the look – slightly damaged IKEA furniture, bought as a stop gap and never replaced. Lots of piles of books, magazines and papers that hadn't quite made it to the recycling. Marked paint on the walls where fingers habitually touched and the wet dog brushed past.

Second, there was another, almost identical house on the same road for sale that was significantly less expensive than the price Annie was hoping to achieve.

We had to pull out all the stops, and quickly. Within a week, paint had been refreshed and there were new cushions and throws on the sofas and beds. Under our supervision, a huge tidy-up operation had been executed. The professional photographer took some fabulous photos, including gorgeous twilight shots, and the house was on the market at £150,000 more than its tired-looking neighbour.

Within a week of the listing going live, Annie called me in tears of joy. They had accepted an offer well above the list price because so many viewers wanted to buy. Annie and her family were able to secure their dream home.

Seven steps to staging your home

When staging a home, there are certain key things that need to be done. These are summarised in my unique, seven-step ADDRESS system:

- Assess
- Declutter
- Decorate
- Re-imagine
- Emphasise

- Stage

- Sell

More detailed explanations of each step are in *Sell High, Sell Fast*, but I will run through them all in broad terms here.

Assess

First, you need to work out who your ideal buyer is and assess what your home is offering them. This is a conversation to have with your estate agent in the first instance. They will have a good idea of the profile of people who have been buying homes like yours in the local area recently.

Do a little homework to assess the competition in your neighbourhood and compare what you have to offer against the other houses your buyer will be viewing. Doing a Rightmove search in your price bracket, as well as the ones above and below, will help you to answer this question.

The next step is to decide how much work you need to do on your home before you have any marketing photos or videos done. The sense of panic this step instils in many of our clients is perfectly understandable – this is your 'lived-in' home. But stay calm. I'm often asked, 'Is my home worse than anything else you've seen?' Trust me, you would have to be in a real mess for that to be the case. Occasionally I've had to drive straight home to shower after visiting a home before heading back to the office. In ten years, I've only had to ask a family to move out before I could help twice.

Take some time to think about and fully answer the following questions:

- Why are you selling?

- Who is your buyer?

- What else is on the market that your buyers are going to be looking at?

- Take photos of your home – what do you see?

- Create a folder of pictures that capture what you are attracted to in the homes you view – what do they have in common?

- How much clutter do you have?

- Does your home have an unpleasant smell? Perhaps ask a friend this one.

- What state are your garden and any outbuildings in?

- Will your exterior decoration prompt a buyer to view or just drive past?

- Does your internal décor appear tired or dated?

- Look closely at your carpets – do they need cleaning or replacing?

You can recruit help with these questions, and write a to-do list if you're feeling overwhelmed.

Declutter

This is usually the hardest stage and must be done before decorating or restyling your rooms. If you commission a decorator to paint your walls to freshen them up, they will charge you considerably more if they have to work around your clutter.

The key tasks of the declutter stage are to:

- Equip yourself with boxes, labels and marker pens.

- Find a friend, or a professional, to help. Decluttering is much easier with a neutral party alongside to help with the decision making.

- Decide what stays and what must go.

- Allocate everything into piles – 'leave where it is', 'keep but pack for now', 'throw away'.

- Book the skip, charity collection or auction. Get the kids to tidy up or collect their stuff if they have moved out but their stuff hasn't.

- Get the 'throw away' pile out of the house and off to its final home.

- Decide whether you have space at home to store your 'keep but pack now' pile or whether you need to find storage off-site.

- Clean and clean again.

Decorate

Now is the time to get the decorator in to paint those walls a neutral colour. The right neutral depends on the current fashion, so do a little research before you buy any paint. Do some patch testing on your walls before you take the plunge, as the light in your home will affect the colour. You are aiming to give the house a subtle, fresh feel to make it appealing to a wide range of buyers.

Some things to consider at this stage:

- Try to find a decorator who can come quickly – it's worth paying a little more to get on the market sooner.

- Take advice on the best colours to attract a buyer.

- Look at your ceilings and woodwork as well as the walls, as they may also need doing.

- Painting one room may make other rooms look tired, so be prepared to do a bit more than you'd planned.

- Don't forget the external woodwork (fascia boards and windows) and especially the front door and the garden gate.

- Be sure to complete any minor repairs you come across.

Re-imagine

You live in your home in the way that suits you. This may or may not make sense to other people. Stand back and remember how the rooms evolved. Consider how someone else may choose to use the rooms. What makes the most sense? What do your likely buyers search for in their keywords on Rightmove as their 'must haves' and their 'would love to haves'?

Some things to think about:

- Does each room have a clearly defined function? Be objective in your assessment of why each room is used for its current purpose.

- Is the function of each room one that is relevant to most of the buyers you believe will be interested in buying your home? If not, you need to rearrange your furniture or rent furniture that will define the function more clearly.

- Check that the flow of your home makes sense. Make sure that the way each room links with neighbouring rooms will appeal to a broad range of people. Now is the time to change things if necessary.

Emphasise

This is the time to decide which lifestyle aspects of your home to show off to anyone viewing online. You want to cleverly emphasise your home's best features and draw focus away from anything that is less than ideal. To do this, consider:

- Which areas are the stand-out features of your home? Perhaps you have an amazing conservatory, a cosy window seat, a contemporary kitchen or a sumptuous bathroom.
- How do you use these areas?
- What do you love about them?
- How can you visually tell the story of these areas to your viewers?

Once you've thought about the above, make a list of what needs to be done and what props you might need to properly show off those spaces.

Stage

Staging is the bit where you bring everything together and put all your props, additional furniture and accessories into place. By the time you get here, you will have decided where you need additional furniture. If you've moved out already, you may be looking to furnish the whole house. If you're still living in your home, you may be adding soft furnishings, accessories and perhaps replacing any tired pieces in order to attract your target buyer.

The key actions and considerations of this step are:

- Collect together everything that you're going to need. If you need a lot of additional items, choose a staging company to work with – it will probably be much more cost-effective to rent these items than buy them.

- If you're staging your own home using things you already have, think about the focal point of each room and about how to create symmetry and balance for maximum effect.

- You may want to seek help positioning things and creating the perfect scenarios in your home. Professional staging companies will do this for you, or you may have a friend with a great eye.

- If you're using a professional and bringing in new furniture, make sure the staging company provides a bespoke solution tailored for your home, not a furniture package.

- Book the photographer to come immediately after the staging is finished so there's no chance of messing things up. Go out for dinner or even to a hotel for the night ahead of the photos being taken. You will need to keep kids and pets out of the way until the photographer has finished.

Sell

Once you've done all your preparation, it's time to mobilise the rest of your team into action. Ensure everything is ready so that when you have agreed on an offer, the sale can progress quickly and you can move on to the next exciting chapter in your life. Make sure you've signed all the paperwork your agent has given you.

Your to-do list at this stage:

- Approve your brochure and your online marketing as soon as the photos come back from the photographer. Make sure your agent uses a professional photographer – there is no point spending a lot of time and effort getting your home looking great if the photography doesn't show it at its best.

- Check in with your agent at least once a week. Be proactive – don't leave it to your agent to call you.

- Ensure you, or your agent, have collated all the documents and information a viewer is likely to ask for.

- Choose a solicitor and let them know you're selling ahead of any offers coming in. If you instruct them early, they'll get your property pack ready with all the necessary forms. This way, everything will be available as soon as you have accepted an offer.

- Keep in touch with your solicitor once you have accepted an offer. Understand exactly what stage the progression of your sale is at and where any hold-ups occur so that you can act quickly to move things along if necessary.

- Start planning your move, whether you have bought somewhere new or you're moving into rented accommodation.

Staging occupied homes

One of our most asked questions is about how staging works in occupied homes. If you are living in your house while you are on the market – the reality for most people – ensuring it stays looking great for weeks at a time can be challenging. It may seem easier to do nothing and hope that viewers will be able to see past all your stuff. You might think your viewers will understand that you are living in the house and that everything will go when you move. They won't. You will hear from agents that viewers don't have the imagination to see past other people's things. My argument is that they can see past your stuff, they just don't see why they should have to. There is a strong argument to say that if you can't be bothered to tidy up for someone who may want to give you several hundred thousand pounds, or even several million, for your house, then they don't want to buy from you. If you don't take the trouble to present your house in an attractive way, your potential buyers will get the impression, subconsciously, that you don't care about them.

When we work in occupied homes, regardless of whether we are decorating or decluttering, adding furniture or simply styling with an owner's belongings, we ensure that the result is liveable, or at least re-creatable quickly. When writing *Sell High, Sell Fast* I came across the wonderful old-English word 'scurryfunge'. I adapted it slightly from its original definition to mean:

> 'To rush around the house shoving things into cupboards and under the beds in the hour between the estate agent phoning and the viewers arriving.'

A good staging professional will help you live with and in the tidy version of your home between viewings. They will make sure you have a set of photos from which you can recreate the immaculate look. They will leave you with boxes or bags to swap everyday items for the 'show home' versions, notably bedding, bathroom accessories and cushions. It's not as hard as you might imagine, but if you have children and animals to consider it is well worth asking your estate agent to launch your property with an open house. Then, if they get it right, you will only need to tidy up once. We'll talk more about open houses in Chapter 12.

Staging vacant homes

Whatever happens, don't list your home empty, with no furniture at all. If you do, you cannot expect to get the best price for it. As we've touched on, buying a new home is an emotional decision. It is impossible to fall in love with an empty house. If you look at the photos of two identical houses side by side, one empty and the other well furnished, the empty one will not hold your attention. In some countries, it is normal to list homes unfurnished. Sometimes the seller will even take the kitchen with them. That is not the case in the UK, so just don't do it. Rooms look smaller with no furniture in them. It's difficult to tell from a photo of a vacant house whether it should be sold for £200,000 or £2million. Blank walls and empty rooms all look pretty much the same. There is a good reason why most developers will create a show home. They know that the return on investment of showing a home fully furnished and properly staged is huge. They simply wouldn't secure sales as quickly or for such high prices if they advertised empty shells.

What are your options if the house you are selling is vacant and unfurnished? Perhaps you have already had to relocate for work or to get the kids into a better school. Perhaps the house was your parents' home and they have gone into a home or passed away. Perhaps you had a buy-to-let and the tenants have moved out. We work with people selling vacant homes for all manner of reasons, as well as with developers building new homes.

CASE STUDY: Furnishing to fall in love with

We had a call from a lovely agent, Nick, in Hampshire. Nick specialises in achieving great sales for homes that have been stuck on the market for a while, and, as such, he is a real advocate of the power of staging. He was taking on a semi-detached Edwardian home in a popular village. It had been on the market with a different agent for about seven months. The owners had already moved out, taking all their furniture with them. It was in a good state of repair and there were no major drawbacks to the house. But it was stuck.

Nick called us and we agreed to furnish it with a target buyer in mind, which he believed was likely to be a professional couple, possibly with young children. Within a week of the relaunch the owners had accepted a full asking price offer for the house. The furniture and the new photos had made a huge difference and attracted a whole new set of people to view. The furnishing had enabled them to understand how the house would work for them and created a strong emotional response to the photos online that simply couldn't be achieved with empty rooms.

You can, of course, stage an empty home yourself. Many of our clients have tried to 'go it alone' before they call us. Buying and installing a large amount of furniture, or even a relatively small amount to fill in the gaps, in the case of a divorce, for instance, is time consuming and costly. Co-ordinating several rooms, blending pieces with what you already have, ordering things that are the perfect size and making sure they arrive in good time is tough. Flatpack furniture is usually quicker and easier to obtain, but then you have the challenge of putting it together (assuming all the bits are there). Once you've done that, you've got to get rid of all the packaging, hang pictures, mirrors and the perfect combination of soft furnishings and accessories. Very quickly you can see how money spent on hiring experts becomes worthwhile.

Staging professionals know how to curate the perfect inventory and pull it together in days not months. You will have achieved your sale while your neighbour, who's determined to do it themselves, is still dithering over whether to buy the sofa from John Lewis or DFS.

How to find a professional stager

The Home Staging Association UK and Ireland is a good place to start when looking for a professional stager, but you should also check out their Google reviews. When you have found some options in your area, have a good look at their websites. Remember, this will be the team you trust to prepare your home to look its absolute best for marketing. Do their photos reflect the look you want? Below are some ideas of questions you may want to ask before you invite them to your home:

- **How do you charge?** This may be by the hour, per project or linked to property value. They may charge upfront or on completion of the sale. This should be clear, and if they work on an hourly rate, you want an estimate of the time involved.

- **How did you get into staging?** You should expect some background in property or marketing; remember, staging is a property marketing tool, not a branch of interior design.

- **What type of projects do you do?** As a seller, you want to know that someone has experience with your type of project. For example, if you need a lot of decluttering, you don't want them to provide evidence of furnishing only new builds. If you have a Victorian manor house stuffed with antiques, you don't want them to be generally working with small homes furnished with flatpack furniture, and vice versa.

- **Can you show me some case studies of properties like mine?** An experienced stager will know that their strongest marketing tools are their case studies and the statistical evidence they have collected from the work they've done. They should be prepared to share all of this with you.

- **What's your lead time for a project?** I would expect a maximum of two weeks from confirmation of quote, unless there's major decorating to be done. Neither seller nor agent will want to wait for a stager to source the perfect sofa.

- **Could you explain your process for preparing a property for sale?** The process needs to be clear and focused on maximising the sale price. A good stager should be able to source decorators, general maintenance contractors, gardeners etc quickly so that nothing delays getting the property onto the market.

- **Is there anything else you can do to make my move easier?** This could be anything from sourcing a removal team to recommending storage facilities to moving you into your new home by unpacking boxes and placing items within forty-eight hours of the move.

Summary

- Home staging is the process of preparing a home for sale to attract potential buyers.

- The goal of home staging is to enhance appeal, facilitate a swift sale and secure a higher sale price.

- Staging before marketing should be considered as integral to the house selling process, whether it is done by the homeowner or by a professional stager.

- Lockdown challenges led to an increase in the use of creative viewing methods like virtual tours and video. The greater scrutiny these allow has heightened the importance of excellent presentation.

- A well-presented home will attract more viewings and viewers are likely to spend more time in the home.

- The UK lags behind the US and Australia in the use of home staging as a marketing tool, but it is increasingly considered in home sales. Recent years have witnessed a doubling of interest in home staging.

- Professional staging services range from consultation only to fully furnishing empty homes.

6
Professional Photography

I n this chapter, I explain:

- The role of professional photography in marketing a house

- Why professional photography is always worth the spend, regardless of the price point of your home

- Why your estate agent or the local wedding photographer are not the best people to take photos of your house

This chapter follows the one on staging for a reason. Even the best photographer can only take photos of what is in front of them. If you are preparing your home for sale, please don't book the photographer without actioning the advice I have given so far.

Why hire a professional?

Surely when you engage the services of an estate agent, you can expect that they will take the photos needed to list your home? They will. Please, don't let them. The majority of estate agents – and there are a few exceptions – are not trained photographers. They are not routinely taught how to take great photos of houses. Some of them may have done additional training, but ask to see the quality of what they can do before you agree to your agent doing their own photos.

You don't need to take my word for this; the evidence in support of getting a professional in, is overwhelming. The Home Staging Association UK and Ireland produces a report each year based on research conducted via their estate agent, developer and stager network. This report has consistently evidenced that properties with good professional photos attract more viewings than those with poor-quality images. In the 2023 report, 100% of respondents acknowledged that to be true.[29] The online agent Strike says that homes with professional photos will sell 50% faster and 39% closer to the asking price than those without.[30]

An in-depth piece of research commissioned by the estate agency Barrows and Forrester in 2023 found that 80% of people viewing homes on the portals would click through to a listing purely because the initial image was appealing. In contrast, those listings with a poor first image could struggle to sell, as 59% of buyers stated they would bypass a property with an unappealing first photo. Once they have clicked through to the full property advert, 71% of buyers admitted that the full range of property images is the first thing they flick through before checking out the written details. And 49% admitted they wouldn't even bother with the rest of the listing if they didn't like the look of the property from the photos alone.[31]

The message is clear. You need to think of listing your home in a similar way to a profile on a dating website. The point of the profile, whether for a house or a person, is to excite interest. It should be carefully designed to tempt someone looking online to get in touch – or, in the case of your house, to book a viewing. What you are trying to prevent at all costs is the instant 'swipe right' reaction when your house listing appears in front of someone with the funds to buy.

Interior photography

Jon Holmes, who has been our photographer of choice in the Midlands for many years, advises that sellers should look at the properties their potential agents have listed and see how they are presented, not only on Rightmove but also on their social media, including their Instagram grids.

As soon as you list your home for sale, viewers will expect to see a selection of interior and exterior shots. It always raises suspicion if there are only external photos – people will wonder what's wrong with the inside. Even if the inside is a disaster, the listing should indicate this, both in the photos and the text. The risk of having no internal photos at all is that you, your agent and potential buyers who don't want a project house will waste an awful lot of time. My suspicion is also raised if there are no external shots. Don't try to hide it if the house is under a pylon or next to a busy road or railway line. Aim for a good mix of internal and external photos.

Don't use a professional photographer to take pictures of your home unless they are experienced in interiors. It doesn't matter how great the photos that they took of your wedding were, interiors photography is a different discipline. It would be like asking a chef from an Indian restaurant to produce an exquisite French meal. They could do a fabulous job, but they may not. If you want French cuisine, get a chef who cooks that type of food day in and day out. If you want great property photography, pay a specialist.

CASE STUDY: Curved walls

My favourite example of using the wrong kind of professional photographer involves a house we staged for a developer in the early days of the business. The experienced developer assured me that they had a photographer who they had worked with many times before and they didn't need me to book the one we habitually used. I agreed, as they appeared to have it all in hand. When we received the photos, I didn't know whether to laugh or cry. The walls of the house, which was a perfectly normal four-bed home with the straight walls of a new build, were all slightly curved. The photographer, lacking the proper wide-angled lens essential for interior photography, had used the 'wide angle' function on his phone camera instead. Try it for yourself, you'll see what I mean. All the walls had developed a slight curve and the bathroom looked as though it was in a round house. When I looked up the photographer online, his events portfolio was fantastic. I would have happily booked him for a wedding, but I won't be adding him to my little black book of great interiors photographers.

One of the advantages of hiring a professional staging business is that they will be working with professional photographers on a regular basis. This has several advantages for you as a home seller. First, they will know who's on top of their game, and what the lead time might be to get them booked in as soon as your home is ready. Just like any other in-demand professional, the best photographers will need a couple of weeks' notice to fit you in. Second, positioning furniture and accessories to their best advantage in photos is an art form in itself; the combined skillsets of stager and photographer will amplify the results.

CASE STUDY: Bed frame vs view

We once staged a new-build home for a local developer who hadn't used our service before. The plot we furnished for him was a lovely five-bed family home with particularly good views from a large triangular window in the main bedroom.

After we had staged the home, the developer called me to question why we had positioned the bed on the end wall of the room instead of facing the big window. I explained that, had we put a king size bed facing the window, which was probably what the new owners of the house would do, then it would be difficult to photograph the room. And on walking into the room, the first thing you'd notice would be the side of the bed, not the fabulous view. Fortunately, the house sold quickly and I was proved right.

Exterior photos

I see some beautiful homes with high price tags but when I look at the exterior photos, I am horrified. Sellers sometimes spend all their time and energy on getting the house ready inside and forget to go through the same process in the garden and grounds. You should do exactly what you did for the interior of your home: get your own camera out, take some photos and then look at them on a big screen. What will the professional photographer be seeing through the lens? Do you need to tidy up, weed the borders, rake the gravel and mow the lawn before they arrive?

The job of the professional photographer is not to take 'happy snaps' outdoors but to showcase the lifestyle your home offers. For example, if your kitchen opens onto the patio through bifold doors you should expect the photographer to take photos with the doors open and the outdoor furniture looking as though you are about to entertain friends in the sunshine. In the winter months, we have successfully created a vibe outdoors around firepits with faux sheepskins and cosy rugs on the furniture. You don't even have to light the firepit, most professionals will be able to photoshop in a realistic fire. Jon Holmes advises that it is worth photographing from the outside looking back into a well-lit interior space, and that 'this works particularly well looking towards a kitchen to offer the suggestion of alfresco dining.'

There is a trend in marketing premium homes for staging a swanky drive with posh cars. If this is relevant to you, it is well worth asking your agent to liaise with the local Ferrari or Porsche dealer to see if you can borrow one of their new models. In a country home, this may be the Land Rover or Grenadier dealership. Your photos are showing off a certain lifestyle.

Even if your home doesn't fit the Ferrari vibe you can, at the very least, make sure the bins are hidden from the lens and that the McDonald's boxes in next door's garden have been removed. Nobody wants to spend their money on a home where the reality of life is shown all too starkly from the outside.

I once heard a story from an American real estate agent about a house being sold on a street where no-one habitually cared for their gardens. All the front lawns were overgrown and untidy. Wanting to achieve the best sale for his client, the estate agent himself paid a gardener to mow all the lawns in the street for the time the house was on the market. I can't yet imagine a UK agent going to such lengths for a seller, but maybe it's worth asking your agent to be the first...

Elevated and drone shots

Professional photographers will have equipment that allows photos to be taken from different angles. Taking pictures from a camera elevated on a long pole gives a great impression of the outside. Do remember though, if your photographer is using a pole, they will be able to see a much wider angle, so talk to them and check if there is anything else you need to move. The last thing you want when you get the photos back is to see that the bins are back in view or the broken fence that you haven't yet had time to mend is visible.

Drone photography is a specialist discipline and requires the photographer to hold a drone licence. As such, not every professional photographer is able to offer drone photography and it may come with additional cost. The homes that benefit from use of a drone are those with land or that occupy a particularly good plot or position surrounded by countryside. If a house has a view, for instance, it may not be possible to capture it in its entirety from ground level. Using a drone will give a 360° view and allow a prospective buyer to understand how the property fits into its surroundings in a much more detailed way. A report by Focal Agent cites statistics that say properties with features that can be shown and enhanced by drone photography are likely to sell up to 68% faster than similar homes photographed without the use of a drone.[32] It is also worth mentioning that sellers shouldn't be seduced by an agent who offers drone shots as standard. Holmes told me: 'There is an agent I know who uses drone shots on every listing, even for properties that don't need them. An example is a new-build site, where all you can focus on in the drone shots is a plethora of neighbouring houses that overlook the garden.'

CASE STUDY: View vs approach

My own home is a great example of a house that does need drone photography to show it to best advantage. I live in a Victorian farmhouse and the barns, as was the case with so many other similar properties, were sold years ago and converted into houses. This means that the approach to my gates is through a small courtyard of barn conversions. I love it because I have the security of neighbours but I know, from many conversations with estate agent colleagues over the years, that this will be a disadvantage when I come to move, because the drive-by won't justify the price tag. Buyers will want a long, leafy, private drive rather than having to go through the barns. Drone photography will show that, in fact, the house has views of open countryside on three sides. There is only one window that faces the courtyard; all the others have completely uninterrupted views of fields and a lake. Fingers crossed that a drone will be able to help when I need to sell.

Ask your agent if they can make a referral to a professional photographer. After staging, it will be the best investment in the sale you can make.

Summary

- Professional photography is essential for effectively marketing a house, regardless of its price point.

- Photos taken by an estate agent, unless they are also a trained professional photographer, never showcase a property to maximum advantage.

- Good professional photos significantly increase online engagement and lead to more viewings and faster sales.

- Exterior photos are as important as interior ones, and attention to detail (like hiding bins before the photos are taken) contributes to a positive overall impression.

- Elevated and drone shots provide unique perspectives for larger properties, especially those with land and outbuildings, and can significantly speed up a sale.

- It is crucial that photography portrays not just a home but a lifestyle, including outdoor spaces and any views.

- The quality of the leading property image on a listing significantly influences viewer engagement.

7
The Role Of Video

When I first started writing this book, the section on video came in the same chapter as professional photography. But the more people I interviewed in the course of writing, the more convinced I became that the role of video in property marketing is now so crucial that it deserves its own chapter.

As such, in this chapter, you will discover:

- Why video is now an essential tool for marketing your home

- The difference between a virtual tour and a video

- The role of short-form and long-form video in attracting buyers

The rise of video marketing

Video has really taken off in property marketing since the pandemic. In the various lockdowns, estate agents and sellers had to think of new ways to sell property to prospective buyers who couldn't physically view a house. WhatsApp walkthroughs done by a seller became normal and the estate agents who didn't habitually present homes via video found their businesses struggling. While video is now the norm, it continues to produce a mixed bag of results. Matt Strafford of Dream Home Films, who specialise in creating high-quality promotional property videos, told me that listings with video drive 403% more property enquiries and sell an average of 50% faster than those without video.[33]

Take a look at some property videos on Rightmove. You will quickly be able to tell which have been done by the estate agent on their phone camera and which have been created and edited by a professional. Strafford says that 85% of viewers expect every video they see to be of TV-like quality, and 77% of viewers will stop watching a video if it is poor quality. It is important that, whatever the source of the video, the quality is high.

Both iPhones and Android devices have great cameras, and there are many apps, both free and paid for, that enable video editing. As you would expect, there are a multitude of YouTube tutorials that explain in straightforward terms how to create and edit video content. As such, a few estate agents have become good at making their own videos, and there are a lot of tools that enable an agent to create professional-looking videos if they invest a little time into learning. Is your agent one of these?

If you find yourself speaking to an estate agent who doesn't advocate either a video or virtual tour of your home, find someone else. Chris England of PVS Media, a professional video business in the Midlands, says, 'In 2023, and beyond, video content for property marketing is not a "nice to have", it's become a "must have". For every property at every level. At every price point.'

The advantages of video

Chris England observes that, since the pandemic lockdowns, estate agents have finally woken up to the fact that their online shopfront, their digital presence, their social media and the property portals are available 365 days a year, twenty-four hours a day. An agent could be marketing to a potential home buyer at 3am, 2pm or at midnight. It doesn't matter anymore.

Video is a big component in allowing people to view a home when it suits them, not when the homeowner, the estate agent and the would-be buyer can get their diaries aligned. This has the advantage for the seller that a good video weeds out time wasters. Simon Leadbetter explains: 'If a house has a good video, the number of actual viewings declines to a fraction of what they might otherwise be. But almost every viewing is a genuine potential buyer.' He describes the 'theatre' of what would happen regularly in the past, where a couple might arrive at the house and know immediately it wasn't right for them. They would go through the motions of looking around and say that they would call later, because good manners prevented them doing otherwise. There is nothing more annoying than spending half a day relocating the kids and the pets, doing a major scurryfunge, followed by ironing the bedlinen and swiftly baking a batch of homemade cookies, only to have the family who arrive for the viewing take one look and say, 'Oh. We didn't realise that the kitchen is open plan. That doesn't work for us.'

A good video gives a viewer an opportunity to explore the house in advance of booking a viewing. This means that less time is wasted, fewer hopes are dashed and the people who do come to see the house are genuinely interested. As both England and Leadbetter say, if video content is used properly then everyone who comes through the door should effectively have already seen the property once. They have done their first viewing online and already have a sense of the space and how the house might work for them. When they arrive in real life, they are already in the market to buy. In this way, the video is a pre-qualifier of someone's buying decision.

A video is also something a prospective buyer can share with their family and friends for their opinion. By the time someone books a viewing, they will have seen a well-presented, high-quality video and may already have the support of other stakeholders in the move – these people have already rationalised their buying decision. The video is a key part of the 7–11–4 approach explained in Chapter 2.

Another advantage of video content is the ability for someone who is relocating, either to an area of the country they don't know well or even from abroad, to view before they travel. As a potential buyer, viewing homes that are geographically distant is time consuming and expensive. Arriving at a house that has been photographed in a way that doesn't show the damp walls or the pylon in the garden is not conducive to a viewer making a speedy, asking price offer. While video shouldn't be a 'warts-and-all' version of the house, it is less easy to hide major flaws on a video tour than it is with good camera angles. England told me that 'people rightly trust video content more than photos because video is significantly harder to doctor.'

From the agent's perspective, video can be a good way to help them make their business more efficient. For a seller, it has the advantage that, if your agent is efficient in their time management, they have more time to help you. That being the case, you can quickly see why it might be worthwhile paying a little bit more

HOW TO SELL YOUR HOUSE

to an agent who uses video not only to advertise your home, but as a tool to manage their own time well.

I spoke to Michael Doherty, who was a co-founder of the UK's first technology-led property marketing platform, ehouse. His view is that an agent shouldn't be rushing to show a property to someone who hasn't seen everything there is to see online first. The more traditional view is that an agent should grab all would-be viewers and rush out to show them a home as soon as they express any interest. Time is so precious these days. How much better would it be to find an agent who manages their own time, your time as the seller and also their buyers' time? These agents will ensure that the only people who come to view your home are seriously interested, well-informed and in a position to put an offer in.

The disadvantages of video

There are some disadvantages to video. It is much harder to hide clutter, poor décor and otherwise bad presentation than it is in a set of carefully angled photos. A good photographer can make sure that personal belongings are moved out of shot for photos or avoid certain rooms and angles; this is not so easily done with video.

All the videographers I spoke to in the course of my research told me that the one thing that differentiates videos that are successful as a part of the marketing strategy and those that aren't, is the presentation of the home. Commissioning a great videographer is not enough to ensure success if the house is a mess. Back to the chapter on home staging then.

From the point of view of a professional videographer, Chris England explains:

'Empty properties are a nightmare. You can't get a sense of scale or perspective. If you're videoing a £2million home or a £200,000 home, it's really hard to tell which is which if they're empty. And yet you have a scale factor of 10, it should be obvious.'

There is also a risk of repetition. When asking your estate agent to create a video for your marketing, make sure your agent understands what you mean. If you look at video tours of homes on Rightmove you will quickly find a few that are just an amalgam of the photos. England's view is that this is lazy marketing. It doesn't add anything to what the potential buyer can learn about your home. It's just a slideshow of your existing photos that have been stitched together. Michael Doherty agrees: 'There is no point putting out something that you call a virtual tour or video just to tick a box. Because unless it makes the property look great then what's the point of it?' The video should add content, not repeat what can be seen in the photos.

You will also need to be prepared to pay for the video as a separate cost if the videographer is not your estate agent.

Another potential downfall is optimisation. Simon Gates of Opening the Gates told me that, these days, about 85% of website traffic is viewed through a mobile device. If your agent's content, whether it's their website or promotional videos, isn't optimised for mobile then they risk losing a huge proportion of your potential buyers.

We recently staged a home that was listed at in excess of £2million. The video the agent had created had been shot in landscape on an iPhone and it was impossible to optimise it for the screen of an Android as a result. Not only should all video content be optimised for a mobile device, but it also needs optimising for both iPhone and Android devices.

Video length

How long a video tour should be is much debated amongst the property marketing community. It is an important discussion, as attention span for consuming video online these days is reportedly 8.25 seconds.[34]

Video can – and should – be used in several different ways, so your agent may record more than one version. Strafford gives some examples:

'Since I set this business up three and a half years ago, things have changed massively with video formats. Essentially, we only used to do the long-form video, which worked great on Rightmove or YouTube. But Instagram and TikTok are huge now. The format of videos on those platforms is totally different. You literally have to take the camera and turn it the other way.'

Your buyers will consume online content in different ways – more about that in Chapter 10 – and attracting the widest possible audience for your house means finding an estate agent who understands how to create content for more than one platform.

Coming soon

The 'coming soon' video has become popular in the last few years. Exactly as you would imagine, this is the shortest format and provides a taster of what's to come. It's a great way to pique interest in a house while all the internal prep is being done. We work with many agents who will record a 'coming soon' video while we are staging a home. They use it alongside an outside shot of the house together with footage of the local area, perhaps a historic town centre, a cosy coffee shop or the park a few steps up the road from the house that is about to launch. Imagine you are relocating to a new town for work; perhaps the whole family is not yet fully onboard with the move. A short video or Instagram reel highlighting the facilities at the local leisure centre for your sporty kids, or showing your friends a restaurant where you can meet them for a fabulous meal once you have moved, can make all the difference in turning dread into excitement.

Short form

A short-form video can be used as the 'coming soon', or it may be the next enticer. Drone footage of the house that's coming to market can help prospective buyers to place it within its surroundings, especially for someone who isn't familiar with the location. If the house is close to the railway station, being able to see this clearly on a video may attract someone who commutes by train three days a week. A country property can often only be seen properly from the air. A drone video will show off the acreage and the view from a new vantage point. It can be hard to orientate stables and barns in relation to the main house from photos, but video is a great tool to do this.

Long form

Chris England warns, 'beware of only having short video clips to showcase your home.' He believes that, while short videos are a great way to get information in front of someone quickly, the retention of that information can be poor. Once the short video or reel has engaged the attention of a potential buyer then having a longer video is essential. Your home is a high-value asset, whatever your price point in the market. To encourage a buyer to part with your asking price, they need as much information as possible.

Anyone who is serious about their purchase will probably want to take more time and have a more thorough walk-through before they book to see it in real life. Doherty suggests 'holding back' the long-form video (or the virtual tour, if you have used that as an alternative) until a potential buyer has expressed a serious interest in the property. This can be a tool to allow the agent to capture more data for the seller on how many people are interested beyond a browse on the portals. If a viewer has to ask for the full video from the agent and the agent sends it to their email address, it opens up the selling conversation at an earlier stage than may otherwise happen. Using a tour video in this way can also overcome any reservations you may have about the security issues of having a tour through your home online.

Long-form videos could be presenter-led; there are some fabulous videos being done this way. A few estate agents are naturals in front of a camera, or have worked hard to look as though that is the case. Personally, I love presenter-led videos – except the ones where it looks as though the presenter is on roller skates. The videos that dash through a home on triple speed with lots of hand waving just make me dizzy.

On the subject of presenter-led videos, Matt Strafford makes a good point about trust:

> 'I think presented live videos are much more engaging than non-presented videos. We're in a world where people have short attention spans. A big part of our job is to create content that is engaging within the first five to three seconds. When you've got somebody talking to you on camera, that engagement goes higher much more quickly. The benefit for the agent is that it builds trust with people who are watching it; they feel as though they know the agent before they've even met them.'

The virtual tour

How does a virtual tour differ from a marketing video? Both are a walk-through of a property but they differ in feel and will appeal to different audiences. A virtual tour of an existing house is created from a camera, set up in different positions within the house. Matterport is currently the most common camera type and you may hear a virtual tour referred to as a Matterport tour. The camera takes photos from different angles in each position and these are stitched together to allow someone viewing online to literally 'walk' themselves through the house room by room. You can jump from one floor to the next and see most aspects of a house in detail; you're not reliant on moving through rooms in an order the videographer has chosen.

The advantage of the virtual tour over a video is that it allows you to navigate easily through a house that has been photographed from multiple angles to produce high-resolution images. Michael Doherty of ehouse explains: 'The virtual tour allows a viewer to go where they want to go. It can be preferable to being taken on a linear, selective journey in a video.'

The possible disadvantage of a virtual tour is that poorer-quality versions are clunky. I still sometimes find myself staring at a ceiling unable to work out which direction I need to move the mouse in to return to a normal orientation. It can also be tricky to see enough detail on a phone screen in a virtual tour which may be a disadvantage for someone who wants to do a quick look on the move. But tech is improving all the time and the good options will produce a tour that can be easily navigated by anyone, with no experience needed.

Summary

- These days, video is critical to showcase your home.

- A virtual tour is a good alternative, or addition, to video as a way of allowing an online viewer to navigate through every room.

- Videos should be of a professional standard, with short clips showcasing the best features for a 'coming soon' or short-form video.

- A longer video could be presenter-led or a more detailed tour of the house.

- You will need different video formats for different platforms.

- Check your video is optimised for mobile viewing.

- The most successful videos and tours show beautifully presented homes – get your presentation right before the videographer arrives.

- Think of professional photography and videography as an investment in achieving the best price for your home.

8
Virtual Selling

Virtual tools for selling homes, both photography and video, have become more common in the last few years. In this chapter you will find out:

- What is meant by virtual selling, virtual staging and CGI

- When these tools might be useful for a home sale and when they aren't

What is virtual selling?

Let's start with some definitions:

- **CGI** (computer generated imagery): a specific technology used for creating art or graphics, which can be static or moving

- **Virtual staging/furnishing**: a digital alteration or renovation of a room, home or property to improve its appearance

- **Virtual tour**: a 3D walk-through of a home that may exist in real life, as explained in Chapter 7, or might have been digitally created based on a floor plan and virtually furnished

When it comes to property marketing, these technologies can be applied in various ways. CGI is a tool loved by developers and architects and can be used to produce high-quality images of a building site, or an individual home that hasn't yet been built.

Virtual staging can be combined with CGI and used in even more situations. A virtual stager often has a design background and is using an inventory of real furniture to stage a home, or a single room, digitally. In many cases, the digital image could be reproduced in real life if necessary. An interior designer might use virtual staging to show what a room will look like once a project is complete, like a more advanced version of the traditional 'moodboard'.

A virtual tour is a walk-through of the house, usually compiled by a Matterport camera or similar. If the house exists in real life, the virtual tour is a real walk-through. If the house is not yet built, the virtual tour can be created from a floor plan and combined with virtual staging.

When is virtual imagery useful in a house sale?

CGIs are particularly useful for selling 'off-plan'. When a developer is looking to attract interest to a new site and generate sales at an early stage, they may produce a set of CGIs. These are getting more and more sophisticated. It used to be easy to tell CGI from real photos but this is less true by the day. In many cases, new developments are being marketed with full house tours and even fly-throughs of the entire site based on digital imagery produced from floor plans and site layouts.

We have become used to CGI in many aspects of our lives. The first film to use the technique was Westworld in 1973. When we watch a film, we know that what we are seeing is not real – we didn't believe that the planet Tatooine was a real place when we saw it in Stars Wars any more than we believed dinosaurs are back on earth after watching Jurassic Park.

I spoke to Tom Durrant of DCTR, who produce virtual images of all types for estate agents and property developers, about the main reasons for using virtual technologies in this industry. He told me:

'There are four main reasons you might want to use virtual staging or CGIs. The first would be planning, to get planning approval to bring to life an elevation or build something that looks photorealistic from a floor plan. The second reason would be for a developer to get off-plan sales. The third is to stage a photo in an empty room, and the fourth reason is to reimagine a space, perhaps a virtual renovation to show the potential of a home that needs work.'

These are all reasons that we recommend virtual staging to clients. Our developer clients will use CGI for their planning and off-plan sales. In specific circumstances, we will recommend virtual staging to our private clients. This tends to be if a room is being used for a particular function but the house would be more functional, and more desirable, if that room were used in a different way. If a house has lots of potential and the renovation is likely to be something the buyer will undertake rather than the seller, then virtual images are useful. We have even used virtual imagery to show how a commercial building would look if it were converted to residential to widen the buyer market.

CASE STUDY: Kitchen in the wrong room

We worked on a gorgeous cottage near Stamford. The owner had moved out to relocate for work, leaving a pretty home unfurnished. Old, beamed properties can look very sad with no furniture and we were asked to physically stage the whole house to attract a buyer. As with many older homes, the kitchen was in a small room and didn't invite modern family living, which both we and the agent believed could be a barrier to getting the best sale. Clearly, moving a kitchen is a big undertaking and not something most people would entertain ahead of a sale. To help a buyer visualise how the house might work much better for them and their family we commissioned digital images of the big sitting room as the kitchen/family room. It completely transformed how viewers thought about the house and a sale swiftly followed.

Durrant explains that if the function or use of a room could differ depending on the buyer demographic, then virtual staging can help show this. He described how they are able to produce a QR code that can be displayed in a room and used to show its alternative uses. For instance, if a room is furnished as a fourth bedroom but could easily be a home office, a nursery or even a gym, upon scanning the QR code the viewer will be able to see how else it could be used. Creating this kind of marketing tool can quickly overcome any objections a buyer might have about the spaces not suiting their needs. Buyers are more likely to make that all-important purchasing decision if they are shown, rather than told, how the house can work for them.

When is it not useful?

We sometimes come across estate agents who suggest virtual staging of an empty house to their client 'because it's cheaper than real staging.' Going for the cheap marketing option in a financial transaction that will affect the rest of your life is never a good idea.

If you are tempted to go along with a recommendation to use virtual images in your listing, think about the first reaction your viewers will have when they arrive at your empty home. Or worse – your cluttered, lived-in home. They have fallen in love with beautiful images online, that's why they booked to view. Then they open the door to a house that looks nothing like the one they have in their minds. Being left with a feeling of disappointment, or even having been slightly conned, won't endear your buyer to you.

It doesn't matter that the listing clearly says: 'These images are computer generated for reference only.' That house had the sofa they've dreamed of owning. It had gorgeous curtains and lots of plants adding life and energy. It wasn't a cold, empty box with grey carpets and white walls; nor did it have '70s-style swirly brown carpet and a dark oak kitchen. The home your viewers want to see is the one they saw in the pictures.

Your estate agent will tell you that viewers know the images aren't real and that they show the potential of the house. Logically, this is true. Emotionally, this is far from the truth. People buy houses based on emotion first. If the emotional connection isn't there, they will tap into their logical brain, which starts to calculate whether they want to make an offer of the guide price or not. Malcolm Gladwell refers to this as 'thin-slicing':[35]

> 'Thin-slicing is not an exotic gift. It is a central part of what it means to be human. We thin-slice whenever we meet a new person or have to make sense of something quickly or encounter a novel situation. We thin-slice because we have to, and we come to rely on that ability because there are lots of hidden fists out there, lots of situations where careful attention to the details of a very thin slice, even for no more than a second or two, can tell us an awful lot.'

However tempting it may be to go along with the agent who says it would be a good idea to do virtual staging or use CGI, don't if your house is empty. In the case of a normal, vacant house, using virtual staging may attract a buyer, but it will only then disappoint them.

Of course, there are people who will buy with their heads alone. They are called investors. They are purely looking for a house that will give them a good financial return. They buy houses to 'flip' – they make money by putting in new kitchens, bathrooms and changing the décor, and they are interested only in the return on their investment. Or they buy houses to rent out. Investors will be able to see past CGI and will make an offer for your house. But they buy low and sell high – it's their business. If you are looking for an investor, then virtual imagery may well help you secure a sale. But if you are trying to sell someone a home, avoid anything that they might consider misleading.

If you do use it, use a professional

If you do go down the route of using virtual images, perhaps to show a different room use or a possible renovation, be careful who you choose to create them. If your estate agent is making a recommendation, then make sure you see the work of the company they recommend before you agree to it. As with anything else, there is a range of quality of virtual imagery. At best, the CGI looks real. It shows beautiful interior design, and the rooms flow seamlessly with an overall theme just as you would expect if you walked into a show home. At worst, you can see the lines where the furniture has been dropped into the photos. Everything looks slightly as though it's floating above the floor and the design element is missing. As AI technology begins to be used in virtual staging, I have heard some horror stories of images arriving where a chair has a leg missing or the wall art has a curtain draped over it.

Sometimes estate agents will suggest virtual staging for homes that are cluttered, need decorating or are only partly furnished. Perhaps one partner has already left because the relationship has broken down, and they've taken furniture with them. These are even worse circumstances in which to go along with the suggestion than if the house is empty. Not only has a potential buyer booked a viewing on the premise that the house looks gorgeous but when they arrive, they are met with something worse than an empty house. The nightmare for most buyers is 'work'. They don't want to have to see past someone else's stuff. They don't want to try and ignore years of accumulated books and magazines, ornaments and old cushions. They are buying a house to take them into the next stage of their life. Most of us don't see an exciting new chapter starting with a vacuum cleaner and a bucket full of cleaning products in our hand.

The virtual, virtual tour

In the last chapter, we looked at the comparative merits of the video and the virtual tour in properties that exist in real life. Another common use for a virtual tour is to show a prospective buyer around a new-build property, where a developer can build a virtual tour based on the architect's plans before the house has actually been built. This is an 'in advance' marketing tool and can show in amazing detail a house that is still just a spade in the ground.

The virtual tour of an unbuilt house is often used in combination with virtual staging. The interior design will be created for each room first and the tour built from the different angles of the virtual photos in combination with the architect's plans.

We also see the virtual tour used in homes that have a problem with their presentation and are not suitable to be videoed for some reason. It may be that the house is cluttered, dated or otherwise not looking its best. A virtual stager will use virtual images and a virtual tour to offer potential buyers a view of what the house could be like under their ownership. If you are in this situation when you are selling, this option is worth considering but as we've touched on, the problem starts when your viewers arrive. As with virtual photos, it doesn't matter how clearly an agent says on the listing that the images have been created digitally, when people arrive, they will still want to see what they saw online. On a logical level, they know this isn't going to happen, but on an emotional level they will still be disappointed when it doesn't.

Good virtual imagery, photos and tours shouldn't be considered a cheap alternative. The investment, in many cases, is not dissimilar to real-life staging. My advice to sellers who call us for a quote and tell me they are also considering virtual staging is to carefully weigh up the advantages and disadvantages of both before committing to either. If the house is real – and by that, I mean not still at plan stage – then real staging combined with professional photography and videography will have a very different emotional impact on a potential buyer to virtual content.

Summary

- In recent years, there has been an increase in the use of digital technology in property marketing, including computer generated imagery (CGI), virtual staging and virtual tours.

- CGI is used by developers and architects to produce high-quality images of a building site or individual homes that have not yet been built.

- Virtual staging is used to digitally alter or renovate a room or home to improve its appearance.

- Virtual tours combine a walk-through of a home with virtual staging. This can be useful for selling off-plan developments or for showing the potential of a property that needs renovation, but isn't ideal for empty or cluttered homes, as it can give potential buyers a false impression of the home.

- It is important for sellers to carefully consider the advantages and disadvantages of real-life staging and digital technology before committing to either.

PART THREE
PROMOTION

9
Listing And Launch

This chapter will help you to:

- Understand what your agent should be doing as the first steps to finding your buyer

- Know what should be included in the listing your agent creates for your home and proofread it from an informed standpoint

At this stage, you have carefully chosen your estate agent and they have done a great job helping you prepare for your sale. Your house looks better than it ever has – a shame to move, really. You have seen the gorgeous professional photos and the videos. Everything so far is showing off the best features of the house and you remember exactly why you bought the house in the first place. Now it's time to see what your agent is going to do with everything you have created between you to find you that choice of buyers they have promised.

Calling the database

I had a fascinating conversation with Elle Wood who runs a marketing agency for estate agents. I met Elle at an event where we were both speakers and was impressed with her take on digital marketing for estate agents. I asked her what an estate agent should be doing first to launch a new property to market. Given her reputation in digital marketing, I was surprised by her response, but it makes complete sense. Elle told me that the first thing a good agent should be doing, long before all the marketing collateral is fully prepared, is calling their database. She said, 'The people that are registered with an estate agent are the hottest buyers. And what you want from your estate agent is the level of proactivity that demonstrates that they have relationships with those buyers.'

Simon Leadbetter agrees. He says, 'Email is the most effective form of sales activation marketing but follow-up phone calls are the most effective form of sales.' He argues that one reason for using a big brand rather than the smaller independent agent might be because they will have access to a bigger database. But it doesn't matter how big the database is if your agent isn't willing to pick up the phone and make the calls. Elle stresses that the agent should be speaking to people who they already know are looking for a house like yours. They should be able to highlight three or four features in your house they know are important to their buyer and discuss price.

Think back to the price triangle in Chapter 4. Your agent will be able to pitch your house to their database of hot buyers at the highest price they think it might achieve, the aspirational point on the price triangle. This is the first opportunity to get feedback on whether the price is right for the market. Are the buyers most likely to be interested in your house, booking to view at that price? Or are they giving feedback that it is a good house but a little on the expensive side? If no viewings materialise from the first calls, emails and the early bird social media post, then when the house is launched on the portals, it should be launched at the slightly lower, more realistic, price. This will ensure the second tier of potential buyers see yours as their dream home. Or you and your agent may agree to use the 'offers over' approach.

The discreet listing

These first conversations that are had when phoning round the database are equivalent to a discreet launch. The house can be sold at this stage, without leaving a digital footprint at all, or it can be listed on the portals later on, without a date stamp that suggests it has failed to sell for a few weeks.

High-value properties are often never listed on Rightmove. The homeowner may prefer to rely on their agent to find a buyer through their network of other agents, including buying agents. They know then that they will only be showing their home to a serious buyer, which can be far less stressful and preserve privacy. As a seller, you might choose this option if you don't want anyone knowing you are selling your house or what price you are looking to achieve.

While you may feel listing discreetly has advantages, unless you are in the super prime market, an estate agent is likely to ask you to consider the fact that a discreet listing will only be seen by a limited number of people. Your best chance at maximising your sale is likely to be good promotion via a combination of the portals, social media and the agent's database.

Portals

In 2024, there are three main internet portals serving the UK market – Rightmove, Zoopla and OnTheMarket.com.

Zoopla says its websites (including PrimeLocation) and mobile apps attract 120 million visits per month.[36] Rightmove was started in 2000. In 2022, its website received over 2.3 billion visits and collectively, people spent more than 18 billion minutes searching for properties.[37,38] This is a staggering statistic.

At any one time in the UK, about 10% of the population are actively looking to move.[39] We know that people start to think about moving several years before they actually do so. They may know they are going to downsize for a long time before it happens. Upsizing for a family is often planned well ahead of the event for example. What this means, is that your house will be seen by a lot of people who are either moving now or thinking about moving soon. If your listing is attractive enough, it may entice some of the 'will move in a year or so' browsers to bring their plans forward.

As well as the dedicated property portals, more general social media platforms can play a role in the launch of your listing. Social media has become a hugely important tool to attract buyers, and agents ignore it at their peril. It seems likely that many people first saw the home they now live in on one of the main social media platforms. In Chapter 10, we'll look at the specific ways your agent can use social media to support your house sale.

Creating your listing

Every property listing needs four things to ensure it is appealing to the widest range of buyers: photos, video or virtual tour, a floorplan and written details. They should all be given equal care and consideration because people process information differently. Some will focus on the photos, some the text and for others it will be the floorplan that excites them enough to book the viewing. We've already talked about the photos and videos; this chapter deals with the written details and the floorplan.

Sales details

Every online listing carries a written description, even if an estate agent no longer produces a brochure. The text will be used on a social media post about a house for sale and your estate agent may send out a letter or email to people they think may be interested as soon as you ask them to sell your home.

I love sales details. It is absolutely beyond my comprehension as to why an agent might feel it necessary to write something like this:

'TWO-BEDROOM TOWNHOUSE IN SOUGHT-AFTER LOCATION – A delightful 2-bedroom townhouse tucked away in a secluded cul-de-sac location with a pleasant outlook.'

The agent has just 250 characters on Rightmove to sit alongside the photo that appears in the search results. Underneath the property name is an icon and a number that tells you how many bedrooms there are. As a potential buyer, you have already sought out the precise location. If the lead photo is of a house that isn't in fact delightful, then all 250 characters are wasted. The only reason now for someone to click through to look in more detail is that this house is cheaper than its neighbours. This isn't the reason you want a buyer to view your listing. That's why the copy is so important.

A game we play in the office sometimes is 'How many "well-presented" homes can you find in 60 seconds?' It's a bit unfair really because we have a local agent who starts every single listing with 'well-presented'. Once I realised this I won every day – until my team cottoned on.

If an agent has a stock phrase or phrases that come up frequently in their property details, you might imagine that they take a look at the property they are writing about and ask themselves if the stock phrase applies. They don't. I have seen project houses with 'well-presented' in the first sentence. Other common ones that take up valuable selling space in the character limit include:

- 'Sought-after area' – it's only sought after if that's where the buyer wants to live

- 'Rarely available' – how is this relevant?

- 'Available to the market' – of course it's available to the market, it's on Rightmove...

If a potential buyer is reading the text, it is crucial that the first words encourage them to click through to read the rest. If an agent wastes this opportunity by saying 'Joe Bloggs estate agents are delighted to bring to market...' then they have wasted over a third of the limited characters they have to draw in the buyer. The first line of your listing, alongside a fabulous photo, should be doing 80% of the heavy lifting of the online marketing of your house.

Go onto your agent's website and read their listings. Would you be tempted by the text to go and view any of the houses they are selling? If the photos were hidden, would the words alone tempt you to book a viewing? Neil Whitfield, estate agency copywriter and author of *The Ultimate Property Listing*,[40] says the purpose of the text is to get anyone searching for a home online, to think 'Yes, that sounds like exactly what I'm looking for.' That thought will mean they click through to the full description to find out more. Whitfield's advice to any agent is that the text must follow through. If the first line mentions the fabulous open-plan kitchen and family room, then once you click through, the rest of the description should be giving more detail about the kitchen and family room. The text shouldn't jump at that point to talk about the garden. Does the description flow well? Does it give a sense of what it might be like to live there?

Windows, doors, radiators, ovens, toilets and wash-basins are standard items in a home in the 21st century.

If a two-storey home is being listed for sale with three bedrooms and an open-plan kitchen/living area, you shouldn't need to say that the house has a staircase. It can be assumed that there is a way to get from ground to first floor. It doesn't take many minutes of scrolling online to bring up a listing that contains the phrase 'stairs to first floor'. How else would someone get to the bedrooms?

Don't even get me started on spelling. If you look at an agent's website and notice spelling mistakes, steer clear. If they don't care enough to check the spelling on a listing that is going live, they don't care enough about how your home is marketed. This may also extend to not caring enough about making sure your sale progresses quickly to completion once you have accepted an offer. As the often-quoted phrase in leadership training goes, 'How you do one thing is how you do everything.'

What is the purpose of the words alongside the photos? According to Whitfield:

> 'The copy can sell a house in a different way
> to the photography. You can go deeper. It's
> almost like when you're reading a good book.
> You're creating the imagery in your own
> mind. Well written copy about a property
> should be encouraging the reader to be doing
> exactly that. It helps them visualise themselves
> wandering round to Jeremy's Deli on a

Saturday morning. You can't do that if you
only have a set of photos to go on.'

The photos and video are what will pull in most people
to look more closely at a property listing. The words
should make them even more enthusiastic. When
a car manufacturer is marketing a new model, how
often do you see 'This new model has four doors, an
engine and some seats'? All that is taken for granted,
and for anyone who needs that level of detail there is a
specification sheet to read. For your house, the video,
photos and the sales details should all tell the viewer
about the lifestyle the house offers, the local area, the
schools, the cafés and the park just along the road. You
can provide a separate 'specification sheet' if someone
wants to check out the number of radiators.

Adding 'wow' to the text

A copywriter in the estate agency industry has such a
hard job. Writing a property description that is hon-
est and exciting is difficult. There are lots of rules to
which an agent must adhere about honesty in selling details. It is, after all, a form of advertising and
so bound by trading standards law. The details have
to sell the house and yet not sound ridiculous. One
house listing that did the rounds of social media in
2022 contained expressions such as, 'A pulchritudinous, grandiose-detailed property.' In fairness to the

author, at least pulchritudinous was correctly spelt. (It means 'beautiful', in case you were wondering.)

The writing of the property description may be a task allocated to the office junior, who is likely working from notes written by the negotiator. They have never seen the house. They may, if they are lucky, have a few photos the negotiator took while they were on site, or even some voice notes from a walk-through. This makes a tough job even harder.

What do the best agents do to make their listings stand out? Some interview the homeowner. Asking the current owner of the house what they love about their home and the area can give a potential new owner a good feeling about their move. This is often seen as something the high-end agents do. Why not do this for every home? It doesn't take long for the agent to interview the homeowner. The conversation, which only needs to be brief, can be recorded as a voice note and transcribed back at the office.

What else? An authentic description talking about features that are shown in the photos is important. If an agent wants to be trusted, a good place to start is the property listing. If it is clear from the photos that the house needs renovation or that the kitchen is tiny then acknowledging this in the description will create trust. Being able to say, 'The kitchen is tiny but look, there is a wall through to the next room which could be taken down to create an open-plan living kitchen,' is much more authentic than saying, 'The kitchen is of a good size in this family home.' For example, Whitfield suggests starting a listing with something like, 'Investors, look at this beauty,' if it is evident there is a lot of work to be done.

With the written description, it's all about providing an interesting, accurate narrative to draw in the right buyer to achieve the best sale quickly.

The floor plan

Every house listing needs a floor plan. It doesn't matter what size the house is, the floor plan is a non-negotiable. To be of value, every floor plan must meet these criteria:

- It must be accurate.
- It needs to have the room measurements and the overall square footage/metres of the house included.
- There should be a compass orientation.
- It should clearly indicate where the main house sits in relation to any outbuildings and the garden.

This section of the book may raise some eyebrows, but it isn't hard for an estate agent to provide this information. Most agents employ someone to come and draw the floor plan for your home. It is often done at the same time as your photos are taken. There are various businesses that will provide professionals to do photos, videos and floor plans as an overall marketing package. If you are paying your agent an 'upfront' marketing cost, you can expect them to be contracting a professional team to take care of these elements and the results should be good.

The more accurate your floor plan, the less likely it is that a would-be buyer will be wasting your time when they book a viewing. A floor plan should answer the questions 'Does it have a south-facing garden?' and 'Can I get a double bed in the fourth bedroom?' at a glance. If these things are important for a buyer, you don't want to spend three hours tidying up in anticipation of their visit only to have them head upstairs and instantly cross your home off their 'potentials' list as the fourth bedroom is clearly only big enough for a single bed.

There are some horrific examples of floor plans on Rightmove. Many don't show the compass orientation of a house, yet using the compass app on a phone quickly answers this question for the draughtsperson. You will find examples of floor plans that don't have room measurements or overall measurements included. This drives me mad. Many buyers want to take their own, much-loved furniture with them when they move. If, upon looking at your floor plan, there is any doubt in their mind about whether their sofa will fit, they will move on to the next house listed.

Accuracy should be a given. Check the doors and windows. I have seen floor plans produced without accurate positioning of doors and windows, even some that appear to indicate the house has no windows at all – and one which appeared to have no way of getting from one room to another.

It's important to have an agent who is proud of the accuracy of their floorplans. As the seller, when your agent sends the property description and floor plan for you to approve, you should check it in great detail. Make time to discuss anything you are not happy with to ensure both you and your agent are satisfied before it goes live.

Summary

- Your estate agent should be utilising their database, calling registered buyers, recognising them as hot leads.

- Your agent should craft a compelling online listing with high-quality photos, videos and an accurate and detailed floorplan to entice potential buyers.

- Listing copy should be optimised by avoiding clichés, focusing on unique and marketable features and having a highly engaging first line.

- There should be consistency in the property description, ensuring coherence from the beginning to the end of the narrative.

- It is crucial to avoid spelling mistakes in the listing – this is as an indicator of the agent's attention to detail in the marketing process.

- The agent must create an engaging narrative to help potential buyers visualise the lifestyle a property offers, collecting as much information as possible from the homeowner.

- For extra 'wow' in a listing, the agent can interview the homeowner to add some authentic insights that will enhance the property description.

10
Social Media Marketing

I n the last few years, social media has become increasingly important when selling anything, properties included. In this chapter, we will discuss:

- Which social media platforms are best suited to your home

- How you can help maximise the reach of your listing

- How agents might be using artificial intelligence to find your buyer

Daniel Daggers, the self-styled #mrsuperprime agent, who has built a hugely successful business based on digital marketing of properties all over the world, told me, 'Any agent who hasn't established a strong personal social media presence in the next couple of years is at significant risk of losing a lot of business to their competitors.' He believes that a company social media presence is no longer enough, that people want to work with people, and potential clients will check out those they might work with on social media.

Which platform?

As technology and consumer dynamics evolve, adopting a comprehensive and targeted social media strategy for each individual property will become the norm. Consumer behaviour suggests that different social media platforms appeal to different demographic groups. An estate agent who is deliberately staying abreast of the ever-changing social media landscape will be able to reach the right target audience for your home and will already have built trust with that audience through their wider marketing. Your buyer is likely to be of a different demographic to you, as the seller. You may have come across your agent via one social media platform, but they will be using others to find your buyer.

In this section, I summarise which platforms are likely to appeal to which buyer groups. I'm sure this chapter, and the comments about AI, will be the reason I'll have to write a second edition of this book in no time.

In response to a 70% surge in interest in the 'benefits of social media marketing' in 2023, Wild PR, a digital marketing specialist, was quoted in Estate Agent Today emphasising the importance of a robust social media strategy for estate agents.[41] You may still come across the local agent who tells you, 'We don't use social media. We know the area and we use our local knowledge and our database to target potential buyers.' Consider this carefully. Why would the person charged with selling your biggest capital asset deliberately choose to limit the pool of people who might buy from you to just the people they already know? The time to use the database strategy is before your house is launched, it's not how you reach the widest group of potential buyers.

The Estate Agent Today article, along with my own experience, offer the following insights to explain the specific tactics estate agents can employ to maximise their online presence. It will give you a basis against which to assess what your chosen agents are doing, even if you are not yet fully confident yourself about the myriad of ways social media can promote your home.

TikTok

TikTok is the newest commonly used social media platform. It has skyrocketed in popularity since its global launch in 2018. As of 2022, it has surpassed 1 billion monthly active users. TikTok's success lies in its short-form video content, especially good for 'coming soon' or 'taster style' videos of houses. The platform is a favourite among Generation Z, with its biggest user demographic being those aged 16 to 24.[42]

TikTok's popularity among a younger audience makes it ideal for estate agents who want to target first-time buyers and those upsizing for the first time. Agents can provide advice on property buying, showcase key properties and offer behind-the-scenes content. TikTok's emerging role as a search engine highlights its potential for addressing common questions posed by potential property buyers. If you are selling a home that may appeal to the TikTok generation, then make sure your agent uses it to its full potential.

Instagram

We have noticed a big increase in the use of Instagram by the agents we work with in the last two years. In the early days, Instagram seemed to be used mainly by individuals for fun but it now has serious business credibility. The largest user demographic is aged 18 to 34. If your home is likely to appeal to a family looking to upsize or a professional couple who want more space, Instagram is a great platform to get it in front of them.

Influencers, brands and celebrities utilise Instagram to showcase lifestyles and products, making it a hub for visual inspiration and marketing. As such, it's a particularly good way to showcase beautifully presented homes. The algorithm doesn't like bad photos, so anything poorly presented or photographed in low resolution risks not attracting much interest. Another good reason to get your marketing materials right.

'Reels' are favoured by the platform's algorithm and estate agents can leverage this feature to enhance the reach and engagement of every home they sell. Reels allow for videos up to ninety seconds, enabling agents to showcase property highlights and conduct quick walkthroughs. The reel format is particularly effective in reaching a broader audience beyond the agent's existing followers – your dormant market?

An agent who is leveraging Instagram to its maximum potential will also be using Instagram highlights. Highlights feature archived stories, and present an opportunity for estate agents to make a strong first impression, organise their content and create a professional look. Using highlights to segment different property types and services helps to create a user-friendly navigation experience. Each highlight should include a unique link, which boosts the potential click-through rate and effectively extends a website onto the Instagram platform.

Facebook

Facebook, established in 2004, is still a dominant force in the social media landscape. With over 2.8 billion monthly active users as of 2022, it attracts a broad age range, from teenagers to older adults, though since newer platforms have emerged, the Facebook user base is slightly skewed towards the older population. If your house is most likely to appeal to someone downsizing, without doubt your agent should be showcasing its features on Facebook.

Another great feature of Facebook became evident during the pandemic lockdowns, when estate agents capitalised on Facebook Live videos to conduct virtual property viewings alongside traditional in-person visits. These brought in substantial daily viewership, and much of the legacy of this period has been absorbed into mainstream property marketing as the new norm. The real-time chat function allows interaction with the audience, answering questions about the property as the virtual tour unfolds.

Agents with a nationwide presence can create regional Facebook accounts. One benefit of this is that someone who is geographically remote from the area to which they intend to move, can do a first viewing on Facebook without having to travel. If someone who has already done a Facebook Live viewing comes to view in person, you know they are probably serious (before you do all that tidying up again).

A social media campaign for your house

If your estate agent is leveraging social media algorithms to target potential buyers, it will involve a strategic approach to reach the right audience with relevant content. The steps might include:

- **Identifying the target audience**: You will have had a conversation about the most likely buyer profile for your house before any of the marketing has started. This is probably the most crucial step to get right with your agent before you begin the process of selling your home, and is especially important for the social media marketing as it may determine the platforms to be used.

- **Using Facebook and Instagram advertising**: Facebook and Instagram offer powerful advertising platforms with sophisticated targeting options. Your estate agent may decide to create targeted ads that showcase your home to a specific audience. Ask if this is part of their marketing strategy.

- **Using geographic targeting**: All the platforms allow location-based targeting. In 2023, most people moved within 16 miles of their current home, up from 9 miles in 2019,[43] so geographic targeting could be a relevant strategy.

- **Creating engaging content**: You will understand by now the type of content your agent will be creating for your home and how you can help make it better. The social media algorithms are especially keen on high-quality video content.

- **Using hashtags**: All the platforms allow users to search via hashtags. Find out which hashtags your agent is using so you can share the listing using the same one to increase the visibility of posts.

- **Optimising for mobile viewing**: Check that any content your chosen agent has on their social media platforms is optimised for mobile viewing.

Your role as a seller

You will likely have social media accounts of your own, as will your family and friends. Utilising your own accounts to comment on, like and share the content your estate agent creates to sell your home will extend the reach of the advertising well beyond what they can do alone. As soon as your agent lets you know they have uploaded another post or video about your home, get in touch with everyone you know and ask them to share it with their followers. You will be amazed at how wide a reach you can achieve with such a simple step. Remember your role as an active participant in achieving the best sale you possibly can. If you don't have any social media accounts of your own, you will almost certainly have family and friends who do. Get them all involved. Elle Wood said to me:

'One of the best ways you can get your property seen is by sharing the post that your estate agent has put out into local Facebook groups. Ask your family and friends, when they see that Facebook post, to share it as well. It's like a ripple effect. If you share it and then someone else shares it, then someone else shares it – it just grows.'

Artificial intelligence

Artificial intelligence (AI) is increasingly being used in the marketing of houses. It can support the social media strategy, hence including here, but it is also relevant to listings and even with the advice on photos.

Daniel Daggers told me – and this is a view I'm hearing expressed increasingly often – that any estate agent who doesn't embrace the positive power of AI will be replaced by those who do. AI will soon be taking on many of the routine tasks done in an estate agent's office. Already, there are multiple ways for an agent to research the market and target new sellers. Many of the Proptech[44] platforms, used by estate agents to help them source new business, use AI to target the dormant market – in other words, to contact people who have been in their homes for, say, seven years or more, to ask them if they are thinking about selling.

Agents can harness the power of AI to create content for social media, blogs and direct marketing. All of this helps an agent market themselves in the local area and can be used to create a compelling narrative about why a buyer might love to live in a particular town. Whitfield told me:

> 'I am using it to help me and my team of writers do the background research and start listing copy. It can do that very well. But then, what it won't tell you is the boots on the ground stuff. That Jeremy's Deli has queues round the corner on a Saturday morning. AI will never be able to tell you that – or not yet, anyway.'

Following on from Tom Durrant's thoughts on using AI to virtually stage homes, Lakshman Mody said in The Negotiator: 'The next wave of AI image editing innovations in residential estate agency marketing is poised to transform how properties are showcased.' He also admits, 'There is still quite a bit that requires a human touch,' and says that physical staging, especially for more expensive homes, still seems to be preferred by estate agents.[45]

If your agent is able to assign many of their background tasks to AI, they have more time to work with you as the seller to help you get your home fully prepared and promoted, and to go out and find you the best buyer. The bit AI can't yet do is replicate the human connections necessary to realise a house sale. That's where your agent will be focusing.

Summary

- Estate agents should maintain a strong personal online presence and engage with potential buyers through social media platforms.

- The selection of social media platforms used to market your property should be strategic and based on your target audience.

- Your agent should create high-quality content, especially videos, that align with the preferences of the target audience on each chosen social media platform.

- Some social media platforms allow geographic targeting that will enable your agent to reach potential buyers within the vicinity of your property. Social media adverts can also maximise your exposure to the target audience.

- All content shared on social media should be optimised for mobile viewing and compatible with both iPhone and Android devices, as a significant portion of potential buyers may view content on mobile devices.

- Sellers can use their own social media accounts to actively participate in the marketing process by commenting on, liking and sharing the content shared by the agent. Encouraging family and friends to do the same will extend the reach of the advertising.

11
Print Marketing And PR

This chapter explains why print marketing is still relevant in a world increasingly dominated by digital marketing platforms. We will discuss:

- Why high-quality print brochures can still be important

- The importance of congruence across all marketing collateral

- When PR can play a role in the sale of your home

The brochure

Given that most properties are now posted online before they appear anywhere else and estate agents are getting better at using social media to promote listings, is there still a place for print marketing?

David Lindley, ex-CEO of Fine & Country and now CEO of By Design Homes, believes that print may actually be more valuable in a digital age because of its relative scarcity. Tom Durrant agrees, telling me that they are finding more people going back to print marketing. In his opinion, people like to have something physical to touch. But he also says that anything printed must be of extremely high quality. Lindley likens this to the experience of buying a high-value car:

'If you go to buy a Jag and there is a tatty piece of paper in the glove compartment instead of a beautiful service brochure then it won't align with the brand and undermines everything that has gone before. It creates a loss of trust between the seller and the buyer.'

An agent selling your home in the prime market might offer you a hardbound book of beautiful photos of your home. This is not only marketing collateral while you are looking for a buyer, but also a souvenir of that house for your own memory box. Lee Armstrong, the managing director of Fine & Country (Midlands) tells me that the brochures they produce for their clients exude luxury and exclusivity. He says both buyers and sellers cherish the physical copies long after the sale as they create 'a lasting impression of a unique and sophisticated experience.'

A physical brochure may be something a viewer of your home will take home with them and show their family and friends to gauge their opinion. If it is of a good quality, then it will positively influence a buying decision. Unfortunately, sometimes the printed material detracts from an otherwise positive impression. Awful A4 details on poor-quality paper with blurred photos, handed to a viewer when they arrive for a viewing, are not going to encourage strong offers.

Armstrong tells me that the purpose of the bespoke twenty-four-page brochures they produce for their properties is to immerse the potential buyer in a visual narrative that 'unravels the essence of all the property has to offer.' The narrative is accompanied by captivating imagery and the homes have often benefitted from professional advice on or help with their presentation ahead of the photographs being taken. Photos typically span two pages, showcasing the unique features of a property. If the photos were poor or the presentation unexceptional, this approach would show every flaw rather than enhance the positive impression of the property. It's a good example of why a marketing strategy has to be joined up.

Other printed materials

There are other print materials that your agent may produce. If you are planning an open day, your agent may create postcards to advertise the event. Or perhaps they send postcards to their database ahead of calling to let them know that your home is coming to market. Whatever goes out must be congruent with the rest of your marketing. A postcard should be on good-quality card showing a gorgeous photo with a few details to tempt someone to come and see the house. Even if yours is not a high-value house, you can still produce a good-quality postcard. There are plenty of online print companies who aren't expensive, even for low print runs. Armstrong says that, 'Personalised postcards serve as exclusive invitations to potential buyers. The tactile experience should enhance the appeal and encourage viewers to come along to the event.'

Some premium agents produce a magazine that they deliver to potential buyers to market their service in a particular area. These magazines are often referred to as 'property porn'. They are designed to have visual and tactile appeal that encourages lovers of property to flick through and imagine their lives in a new home. If you are selling in the premium market, ask how your agent uses print marketing to attract potential buyers who would only be encouraged to move if their dream home came to market.

Advertising in local or national publications hasn't gone away completely. The nationals tend to be the domain of the premium agencies because of the high cost and the target demographic for the homes. Monthly glossies such as the 'Life' magazines may still advertise local properties. My observation, as always, is that these homes are often poorly presented. What's the point of spending a lot of money advertising something that looks untidy, dirty or simply unappealing?

The role of PR

PR, public relations marketing, is different to other forms of marketing and often considered the domain of bigger businesses than a local estate agency. National estate agents often have a dedicated PR department, and some smaller ones use an external provider to help create interesting stories about a particular home or local trends and news that might affect the property market.

The advantage of PR is that the content produced will be read by a different audience to those scrolling on the portals, and perhaps someone who wasn't intentionally looking to move home might be tempted to pick up the phone and book a viewing. We had the experience of working alongside David Lindley's team at By Design and Viv Onslow of The Oracle Group, their PR agency. Viv crafted a compelling write up of a home that had been the wartime posting of Richard Adams, the author of the best-selling children's book *Watership Down*. The house was unique and yet may not have appeared on the search list of a home buyer looking for a country home in that area because it was classed on the portals as 'link-detached'. One wall was attached to what had, historically, been the stables of the house. Lindley explained:

> 'Someone searching for a country manor
> is likely to be put off by the annotation of
> "link-detached", however by getting the
> property to appear in *The Times* and *The
> Daily Mail* you reach a whole new audience
> who would otherwise have never seen
> that property.'

Onslow told me that the advertising value of a home that appears as a story in a national paper is worth three times as much as it would be through a standard advert because there is a perceived third-party impartiality. Russell Quirk of ProperPR agrees:

> 'PR is not advertising – it's better than that
> because it's other people talking about you. PR is
> complementary to social media, email marketing
> and advertising but is the most credible and
> trust-building of all channels and should not
> be underestimated in terms of its power and
> credibility. It provides the biggest ROI of all.'

Summary

- Print marketing can be considered as an addition to digital. In some circumstances, print is more valuable due to its scarcity.

- There is a trend of people returning to print marketing for its tactile appeal.

- High-quality printed materials must be aligned with the brand and the overall marketing package to build trust.

- High-quality brochures in prime property markets can serve as both marketing collateral and a lasting souvenir of a home.

- Well-crafted print materials, such as brochures and postcards, positively influence buyers and enhance property impressions.

- PR can play an important role in property marketing, with the ability to reach a different audience through compelling stories in publications.

12
Viewing Strategies

T his chapter talks about different viewing strategies your agent can use. But surely a viewing is
just a viewing? A potential buyer calls the estate agent,
the estate agent calls the seller and asks, 'Are you in
at 2pm?' and the buyer heads on over and that's that.
Not necessarily. In this chapter, you will learn:

- How the person accompanying the viewer can
  affect the outcome

- Why an agent might use an 'open house' strategy
  to show your home

- What you can do to help your agent get an offer
  from a viewing

Accompanied viewings

A survey published by the Bath property agents Madison Oakley says that buyers feel uncomfortable when the owner is around, and that almost 50% more offers are achieved from viewings with agents.[46] That sounds like a pretty good reason to leave it to the professionals.

As the homeowner, you will know all the niggly repairs that need doing. You will know the things about the house that are inconvenient or the work you would do if you were going to stay. Most homeowners, once they have built a good rapport with the viewer, will find themselves over-sharing these details. You don't want to find yourself explaining how you have to kick the back door at a certain angle to make it open in the winter. Nor do you need to share that, if you were staying, you would put new drainage into the drive because heavy rain floods into the utility room.

Leave the viewing to your agent; they will sell the dream. A good agent will ask you to fill in a property information questionnaire when you sign up with them. Give as many details as you possibly can. This is the information your agent will use to answer all the questions your buyer asks once they have fallen in love with the house.

When your agent says they do accompanied viewings, check how easy it is for a potential buyer to book a viewing slot. If the agent is unable to do viewings outside normal office hours, there is a high chance that, while struggling to find a mutually convenient appointment, your potential buyer will still be scrolling through other properties online. You risk losing them altogether. Remember, if you get all your other marketing collateral right, then your viewer is already about 70% convinced that yours is the property for them. They've seen the photos, they've watched the videos and now, they want to view to confirm their thinking and hopefully make a sensible offer. The way the viewing is conducted is more important than ever.

CASE STUDY: Unanswered questions

Dan was a cash buyer looking for his first home. He had a good budget, having owned a small rental property for several years, which he had sold. He also had agreement on a mortgage in principle should he need additional funds.

A local agent had a three-bedroom semi-detached house listed which piqued Dan's interest. He felt he could afford to buy the house with cash and take out a mortgage once he had moved in to allow him to get some work done on the dated interiors. The house had good potential for adding an extension in the longer term. Dan was keen. The property was empty, the owners having moved away. Dan called the agent. 'We haven't got anyone who can show you round until a week on Saturday.' While disappointed, Dan was keen enough to wait.

On arrival at the house more than a week later, the agent opened the door and ushered Dan in. She told him to, 'Go and have a look. I'll wait here.' Dan went in and immediately questions popped into his mind. He asked the agent, 'How old is the boiler? When were the windows replaced? Who owns the broken fence in the garden?' The agent looked confused, 'I don't know. You'll have to call my boss on Monday.'

Dan didn't call the boss on Monday. He went back to Rightmove to look for another house.

The open house

In the US and Australia, launching a home to market with an open house event has been a common strategy, often the only strategy, for a long time. In the UK, it is becoming a more popular option,[47] and it is definitely something to discuss with the agent you choose to list your home.

The advantage of the open house is that, in the best-case scenario, you only have to tidy up twice. Once for the marketing photos to be done, and once for the open house itself. All your efforts at presentation, keeping the house tidy, sending the dogs to kennels and the kids to friends, can be focused. You won't have to do the endless scurryfunge as your estate agent calls at 10am on a Saturday morning warning of a viewing at 2pm. You can even go down the traditional route of baking and putting on the coffee. We have clients who get the local bakery to deliver fresh-baked treats just as the first viewers arrive. You are selling your biggest capital asset – the price of a few buns is nothing as an investment.

The open house does have to be closely aligned with the pricing and promotion of your home. Your estate agent will want to get as much interest as possible in a short time. Usually, the photos and video are released three to four weeks ahead of the event. Your marketing collateral, when cleverly used, can have dramatic results.

Competition from several interested buyers is what will get you the best price straight from the event, so your agent will be keen to get as many people there as possible. The price is likely to be set at the 'offers over' price for an open day. You should ask your agent how they qualify viewers who want to attend the event – in other words, are they doing any funding checks before someone books? Are they making sure the viewers are 'proceedable' – estate agent language for already having an offer on their own house or being in rented accommodation. These pre-qualifying checks will keep out the nosy neighbours and Sunday-afternoon browsers. The downside is that this may put off any-one in the dormant market who is only thinking about moving because they love your house. Chat to your agent, see what they think.

CASE STUDY: Opening the door to offers

My first experience of the success an open day can create was with a house that had been on the market for over two years with no significant interest and several price reductions. It had been on with several different agents, all of whom had failed to initiate much interest. A big part of the problem was that, although it was a period home and looked great from the outside, the couple were going through an acrimonious divorce. The house was a mess inside, some of the furniture had been taken by the wife when she moved out and the smell in the house was awful.

We decluttered the whole house and brought in additional furniture, soft furnishings, artwork and accessories to create bedrooms in rooms previously used for storage. We cleaned and cleaned again to get rid of the smell. The house was relaunched with new photos and a video for an open day hosted by the new agent. From having no interest at all, the agent found himself showing forty families around on one day. The offers flowed in and a week later a sale was agreed at 20% more than the 'offers over' guide price.

Summary

- Statistical evidence supports the effectiveness of agent-led viewings. It's better if the owner isn't around. Ask your agent to do the viewings and trust them to highlight all the positive aspects of your home.

- The agent conducting the views needs to be equipped with as much information as possible about the property, so that they can address potential buyer questions quickly to facilitate a successful sale.

- Some agents will use open house events. The advantages of this for the seller include minimising the need for multiple tidy-ups. An open house should be aligned with the overall pricing and promotion strategy.

- The agent and seller should be as flexible as possible in accommodating viewers at times convenient for them, including outside of normal office hours. This will enhance their experience and increase the likelihood of a successful sale.

- Collaboration is key. Provide support, act on feedback and advice where possible, and actively engage in discussions with the agent to help achieve a good result.

13
The Timing Of Marketing

N ow that you have created the perfect listing for your home, the promotion aspect of the marketing kicks in. How on earth are you supposed to unravel all the advice from friends, estate agents and the media to get the best possible sale for your home within the timeframe that you want to move in? In this chapter, we'll answer the following questions:

- To what extent does the timing of your launch affect the sale?

- What's the difference between a hot and cold market?

If you don't have any flexibility in your timing, this chapter won't be as relevant, but it still contains useful advice for a future move.

Getting the timing right

Buying a house is an important life goal for many people in the UK. According to one survey, as many as nine out of ten people aspire to home ownership.[48] One result of this is that there is a huge amount of information, and misinformation, about the housing market around. It's a topic much loved by the press and accurate information can be hard to separate from the hype.

Seasonal trends

Historically, there have been widely acknowledged seasonal trends in the housing market in the UK. It makes sense that there are fewer buyers around when Christmas is looming or everyone is away on holiday in the summer. What does this mean for the timing of your sale?

Agents will tell you that spring is a good time to be selling. Psychologically people tend to start to feel more enthusiastic about life again in the spring. The long nights of the winter months don't encourage anyone to go out of the house to view a potential new home. The flip side is, if everyone waits until April or May to put their home on the market then these months will see a glut of new homes on the portals. Your home may be one of fifty available in the right location and price bracket for your target buyer, rather than one of twenty in the quieter months. If there are more buyers coming out of their winter hibernation, then proportionately this may be fine; or it may be that your listing gets fewer views because there is more choice.

The Boxing Day boom is another well-known seasonal phenomenon. The conversation about whether it is actually a good time to launch a house to market is one of the fastest ways to spark an argument amongst a group of agents. The argument in favour of listing on Boxing Day says that while families are at home together, they are more likely to have time to look at properties online. They may begin a conversation about the year ahead. If one of their aims is to move house, they could start browsing as soon as the turkey is cold. Anecdotally, the Christmas holiday period is also a time when divorce lawyers suggest couples are most likely to decide to go their separate ways.[49] Being in close proximity for a week will bring to the fore family tensions and exacerbate them to a point where a big decision is finally made. Taking all this into account, it is easy to see why Rightmove produces stats every year showing a huge spike in traffic to their site on Boxing Day. The agents in favour of maximising this opportunity will tell you that if you come on as a new listing that day, you are almost guaranteed to have a sale agreed early in the new year.

The counter argument is that people on the portals over Christmas are window shoppers. They are simply looking for something to do that doesn't involve another game of Monopoly with Auntie Maud or watching Love Actually for the hundredth time. Our national obsession with property means that the portals are regarded as a source of leisure entertainment. Browsing unaffordable dream homes allows us to imagine a life far away from the reality of hounding the children to load the dishwasher or looking for a turkey curry recipe for the leftovers. Some agents argue that anything listed on Boxing Day will be seen but by people who are not serious about moving. They will tell you that it is a pointless exercise to list at a time of year when you are already stressed about present shopping, making up the spare room for Uncle Tom and fixing the tree lights. If you do list, you can't put up the Christmas decorations until after your photos have been done or your photos will date quickly.

Our experience of working alongside homeowners would generally suggest avoiding the school summer holidays, if possible, if you are selling a family home. Apart from that, I'm not sure it makes much difference what time of year you launch. If you want to sell, do your preparation, create the million-dollar listing and get on with it. There are always sellers and always buyers around.

Hot and cold markets

Our housing market is a big part of the economic wealth of the UK. As such, it is sensitive to political and economic events around the world. In recent years, prices rose quickly as we came out of lockdowns and everyone wanted to move out of the city. They went back down as the post-pandemic economic recovery began to squeeze budgets and interest rates and mortgages went up. Outbreaks of war, which we have seen in recent years, always have an effect on the world economy and, by extension, the housing market.

You may hear your agent referring to 'hot markets' and 'cold markets'. They, and the property press, will refer to the market as heating up or cooling down. This can be confusing. Should you be selling in a cold market or should you wait for it to heat up again? How long will that take?

The hot market

Estate agents refer to a housing market as 'hot' when property is generally selling quickly and house prices are high and rising. In a hot market, there tend to be more buyers than sellers, and so every property on the market becomes desirable or 'hot'. You might also hear this described as a 'seller's market' because the conditions are favourable for selling.

The most recent hot market the UK experienced began immediately after the first Covid-19 lockdown in 2020 and continued until late 2022. The impact of being stuck at home for weeks unable to go outside, except for specific reasons, meant that people reassessed their homes and found them lacking. It suddenly seemed that everyone was selling up and moving to Cornwall.

There was a huge upsurge in buyers looking for more outside space, home offices and even space for a gym at home. Houses that had previously been unfashionable sold within minutes of being listed, in spite of their obvious flaws. Single-glazed sash windows, primitive plumbing and an absence of wall insulation ceased to be an issue when balanced against a big garden and an extra bedroom that could be converted into a home office. Demand for homes outside the big cities went mad, with one study by Urban Architecture in November 2020 reporting a 65% increase compared to late 2019.[50]

In a hot market, house prices rise. We have seen this many times in the UK. The boom-and-bust market of the late '80s and early '90s was an earlier notable example. Something to note if you are selling: even in a hot market, prices don't rise evenly across the country, there are still pockets of regional variance.[51]

How important is the preparation stage of your sale in a hot market? Surely, if the market is buoyant then you will be able to sell regardless? You will. Absolutely. The point of doing the preparation is not to get a sale in a hot market; it is to get the very *best* sale that you can. In a hot market when there are a lot of buyers around, the point of the preparation is to beat the competition. Your agent may tell you, 'Don't bother. It's unnecessary time wasted and an expense you don't need.' We have seen many examples of this not being the case. The preparation our clients have invested from a time and financial perspective has always paid off.

CASE STUDY: A hot sale

Mid-Covid, we were asked by an agent with whom we work regularly to look at a property he wanted to bring to market. The house was in a nice village in the East Midlands and the sellers were moving to Cornwall. They had been able, like so many, to switch their working model to work from home. The area they were moving to was significantly more expensive than the village they were moving from and so they needed to maximise their sale.

They had built a lovely new family room in their house as an extension, which had, unfortunately, been flooded when a water pipe burst. The sellers were reluctant to spend any money on furnishing once the repairs had been completed as, by then, they had decided to sell.

We furnished the family room and helped the owners tidy and style the rest of the house before having professional photos taken ready for their launch to market. The total cost of our help was £6,000, less than 0.6% of the guide price. Within four days, the sellers had accepted an offer of 11.4% over the asking price, more than £100,000, and were able to afford a house in Cornwall that they had thought was out of their reach.

This house would have sold quickly without our intervention, but by taking care of the presentation ahead of the listing, it quickly attracted competing offers. This made all the difference to the final sale agreed. Achieving the best sale in the Midlands facilitated a better buy in the more expensive region of the country.

The cold market

A cooling or cold market is one that is slowing down or where houses are slow to sell. There are fewer buyers than sellers and so the buyers have the upper hand when it comes to making an offer. Sellers are pitching their homes to a more limited pool of people. You may also hear it described as a 'buyer's market'.

In a cooling market, house prices may be falling. How quickly they fall will vary by region, and how long they fall for will depend on the trigger for the fall. There was a lot of press after the especially hot market of the early 2020s about a falling market. Everywhere you looked there seemed to be doom and gloom about an impending recession coupled with a housing market crash close in scale to the one we experienced in the global financial crisis in 2008. This kind of press can, to an extent, create a self-fulfilling prophecy. If people who may otherwise be keen to sell their home decide, on the basis of negative press, to wait a while, there will be fewer buyers and sellers around. Fewer buyers mean lower prices.

Good preparation of a home for sale is crucial in a cold or cooling market. It may well be the difference between achieving a sale and not. In these circumstances, it isn't so much about pushing the price beyond the guide price as it is about achieving a sale at all. If you are already at risk of having negative equity in your home, then launching to market without doing your preparation would be madness. A cooling market is also a time when you need to really listen to and take your estate agent's advice on price. You may want to sell at the same price your neighbours achieved twelve months ago, but the market was different then.

The price at which you sell is contingent on the number of buyers around and the current state of the housing market in your area. Talk to your estate agent; if you have chosen wisely, you have to trust their advice.

When should I sell?

Should you be choosing to sell in a hot or a cold market? Most people don't have the luxury of choice and it can be hard to predict if and when a change may be coming. An invasion on the other side of the world can flick the switch from hot to cold overnight. It's similar in many ways to playing the stock market. Property investors may be able and willing to hold onto cash at a time when they think prices will be falling in order to buy something as cheaply as possible. Most of us, when we are considering a move, don't have that choice. As long as you are buying and selling in the same market, your money is worth the same in a cold market as it is in a hot one. If you sell at a time when the price of your house appears to have fallen from the previous year, you are probably not losing anything in real terms if you are planning to buy straightaway. The price of the house you are buying has likely fallen by a similar amount and your money will still have the same relative value.

A problem arises if you have bought in a hot market and need to sell in one that is falling within a relatively short space of time. This is one of the factors contributing to a complicated post-pandemic market. There are many homeowners who bought at the top of the market. They escaped city life when they didn't need to be in the office and the children were being home schooled. As things normalised again, and the inevitable return to the office and real-life school occurred, the Northumbrian coast began to feel a long way from London for many people. Rural life can lose its romantic appeal in the winter when the mud is relentless, however gorgeous the view. Single-glazed windows and Victorian plumbing are less charming in everyday life; they are inconvenient and expensive. For families who have found their true dream home and are fully committed to life without a Waitrose for fifty miles or a decent coffee shop a few steps from the front door, this isn't a problem. For those who found their dream turning rapidly to a nightmare, the price at which they bought their new home was significantly higher than the price they can now hope to sell it for.

Whenever you sell, don't risk coming to market under-prepared at an over-inflated price. Selling your home is hard enough, don't tie your hands behind your back before you start.

Summary

- There is a lot of information about the property market but it can be misleading. Press coverage creates hype, making it challenging to discern accurate information. Political and economic events influence market conditions.

- Historically, there have been seasonal trends but there is always a counterview.

- Spring is widely considered a good time to sell and is worth considering if you want to show off your fabulous garden.

- Boxing Day sees a spike in online property searches, but opinions differ on the effectiveness of launching on this day.

- A hot market is characterised by quick property sales and rising prices. There are more buyers than sellers, which can create competition for every house listed. Preparation is crucial in a hot market to increase competition and secure the best sale.

- A cold market is a slower market with fewer buyers than sellers and may be characterised by falling prices. Effective preparation becomes vital in a cold market to increase chances of a sale.

- Listening to your estate agent's advice on pricing is key, especially in a falling market.

- Overpricing and under-preparedness will hinder your sale and may even stop it happening altogether.

Conclusion

My promise to you at the beginning, was that by spending the time reading the book you would gain an understanding of basic marketing theory and how it applies to the sale of your home. I set out to explain the role of home staging, why you need professional photography, videography and a social media strategy. And I promised that by the end of the book, you would have learned how to find the right estate agent and would be clear about your role as a key player on team 'sell my house'.

I hope in reading you have gained all of this knowledge and feel equipped to enlist the right people to help you not to sell, but to maximise your sale, so that you can move on to the next phase of your life having realised the full potential of your largest capital asset.

Selling a home in the UK is difficult and complex, made more so by the lack of obligatory licensing of estate agents. However, in researching and understanding the complexities and playing an active part in the process, you can become the manager of a high performing team. Your role is to find the agent with the best marketing strategy for your home. Here's a recap to keep in mind:

- Curb your instinct to list with the agent offering the highest valuation and lowest fee.

- Remember the pricing triangle and the strategy associated with each price point.

- Make sure your home is staged, either by you or professionally, to showcase the lifestyle of your target buyer.

- Highlight this lifestyle with great professional photos and a video.

- Make sure your agent has a strong viewing strategy. An open house is a really good way to generate competition amongst buyers.

- Understand how you can help promote your home by connecting with your estate agent's social media strategy and sharing content to spread it much further through a target audience.

By preparing yourself for the process, as well as your house, you will find yourself able to move into the next phase of your life with enthusiasm rather than dread.

Good luck!

Appendix

The dos and don'ts for selling your house

As I was interviewing people for the different sections of the book, my last question to each of them was: 'What advice would you give to your best friend about how to choose the right estate agent to help them sell their home?' I collated their responses into a big list of dos and don'ts that I hope will help you in your home-selling journey.

Dos

The following are things you should do *before* you invite an agent to visit your home:

HOW TO SELL YOUR HOUSE

- Ask for recommendations from friends who have sold locally recently.

- Have a good look at the agent's website as well as their listings on Rightmove.

- Ask them to send over evidence of the houses like yours they have sold recently.

- Use the information on GetAgent, Zoopla and Rightmove to check they are actually selling houses, not creating listings that don't sell.

- Check how many price reductions they have – are they listing high to get business and then reducing quickly?

- Have a good look at their social media accounts. Are they active on social media? Are they using their accounts to actively promote their listings? Do they appear knowledgeable about the local area and the local housing market?

- Read their property descriptions carefully – would you go and look at their listings based on the way they describe a house?

- Is there a floor plan for every house they list? Is it of a high quality?

- Look at their photos. Are they of a high quality? Have they clearly given advice about the best presentation before allowing the photographer through the door?

- Look at their videos. Are they maximising the use of video to sell their properties and tailoring video content to a target demographic?

- Check out the local houses that will be your competition when you launch. What are they offering compared to yours? Also check the ones that are listed a little higher and a little lower than you expect yours to be.

Then, at the market appraisal appointment, you should ask these questions:

- What will be your marketing strategy?

- What properties have you have sold like mine in this area recently?

- What is your listing to completed sales ratio?

- Is there a fixed contract term?

- Do you charge an upfront marketing cost?

- What do you think is the likely profile of my buyer?

- How will you ensure that my house is presented as well as it can be to attract my target buyer?

- Is there any work you think I should do ahead of the marketing?

- How will you promote my home to the target buyer?

- What happens if we don't achieve the guide price within the first six weeks?

- How will you use video to promote my home?

- Do you use a professional photographer? Is that a separate cost?

- Who conducts the viewings? Do you do viewings outside office hours?

- Will you use an open house event to launch my home to market?

- What do you think the guide price of my home should be? What is your evidence for that valuation?

- What is your fee? Do you work on a sliding scale fee structure?

- How will you negotiate with potential buyers to make sure I get the best possible result?

- How will you make sure my sale progresses smoothly to completion?

- Will you create a WhatsApp group including the other professionals we will need involved so that we can have transparency as the sale progresses?

Remember – great service doesn't come at the cheapest cost. Be prepared to pay your agent an upfront amount for the professional photos and video and a fair fee for the work they will be doing on your behalf.

Don'ts

Below are some things you shouldn't do, if you want to maximise your sale:

- Choose your agent based on the highest valuation and lowest fee.

- Go with an agent who wants to get you on the market as quickly as possible without considering the preparation that may need to be done.

- List with an agent who can't give you clear answers about their strategy to market your home to a defined target audience.

- List with an agent who wants to tie you into a lengthy contract.

- Instruct someone who can't produce evidence of other homes like yours they have sold in the local area recently.

- Go with someone who can't produce their completion figures relative to their listings. It is important that you know they can achieve sales, not just listings.

Selling your home is emotionally and practically tough. But it is also the gateway to an exciting new stage of your life. Good luck, and please get in touch if you would like to chat more about how to sell your house.

References

1   E Penhaul, *Sell High, Sell Fast: How to sell your home for the best possible price in the quickest possible time* (Rethink Press, 2020)
2   A Cutmore, 'Revealed! How often the average Brit moves house', *Ideal Home* (10 May 2022), www.idealhome.co.uk/news/zoopla-average-brit-moves-home-181281, accessed February 2024
3   The Office for National Statistics, *UK House Price Index: December 2020* (ONS, 2021), www.ons.gov.uk/economy/inflationandpriceindices/bulletins/housepriceindex/december2020, accessed February 2024
4   M Da Silva, 'Market share of self-employed agents is growing fast' (Property Industry Eye, 28 November 2023), https://propertyindustryeye.com/market-share-of-

self-employed-agents-is-growing-fast, accessed
March 2024

5   TwentyCi, 'Property and Homemover Report
End of the Year 2023 Summary' (no date), www.
twentyci.co.uk/phmr/twentyci-property-
homemover-report-q4-2023, accessed March
2024

6   Ipsos Mori, *Veracity Index 2023: Who do we trust
the most?* (no date), www.ipsos.com/sites/
default/files/ct/news/documents/2023-07/
Veracity%20Index%202023.pdf, accessed
February 2024

7   A Kerr, 'Estate agent fees – and how you can
save in 2024' (HomeOwners Alliance, no
date), https://hoa.org.uk/advice/guides-for-
homeowners/i-am-selling/how-much-should-i-
pay-the-estate-agent, accessed March 2024

8   Propertymark, *Annual Report and Financial
Statements for the Year Ended 31 December
2022* (no date), www.propertymark.
co.uk/static/27a50d49-c359-4d14-
b4f6630489a99022/2c6fab10-3a6b-4491-
9222db63f2636283/propertymark-annual-report.
pdf, accessed February 2024

9   Propertymark, 'Regulation of property agents
around the UK' (no date), www.propertymark.
co.uk/professional-standards/uk-regulation.
html, accessed February 2024

10 UK Government, *Estate Agents Act 1979*, www.
legislation.gov.uk/ukpga/1979/38, accessed
February 2024

11 UK Government, *The Consumer Protection from Unfair Trading Regulations 2008,* www.legislation. gov.uk/ukdsi/2008/9780110811574/contents, accessed February 2024

12 UK Government, *The Consumers, Estate Agents and Redress Act 2007,* www.legislation.gov.uk/ ukpga/2007/17/contents, accessed February 2024

13 UK Government, *Data Protection Act 2018,* www. legislation.gov.uk/ukpga/2018/12/contents, accessed February 2024

14 N Hopkirk, 'How long does it take to sell a house?' (Zoopla, 19 October 2023), www.zoopla. co.uk/discover/selling/how-long-does-it-take-to-sell-a-house, accessed March 2024

15 Rightmove, 'House Price Index' (February 2024), www.rightmove.co.uk/news/house-price-index, accessed March 2024

16 S Godin, *Purple Cow* (Penguin Books, 2005)

17 P Kotler, *Marketing Management: Analysis, planning and control* (Prentice Hall, 1972)

18 S Godin, 'The difference between marketing and sales' (Seth's Blog, 29 May 2009), https:// seths.blog/2009/05/the-difference-between-marketing-and-sales, accessed February 2024

19 J Lecinski, *ZMOT: Winning the zero moment of truth* (Think With Google, 2011)

20 J Durrant, 'Propertymark and RICS must overhaul sole agency agreements' (The Negotiator, 29 January 2024), https:// thenegotiator.co.uk/blog-propertymark-and-

rics-must-overhaul-sole-agency-agreements,
accessed February 2024

21 J Durrant, 'Propertymark and RICS must
overhaul sole agency agreements' (The
Negotiator, 29 January 2024), https://
thenegotiator.co.uk/blog-propertymark-and-
rics-must-overhaul-sole-agency-agreements,
accessed February 2024

22 Aston James Associates, 'What are RICS
valuations: What you need to know about
valuing your home' (2022), https://
ajasurveyors.co.uk/what-are-rics-valuations-
what-you-need-to-know-about-valuing-your-
home, accessed February 2024

23 KCM Crew, 'How To Get The Most Money
When Selling Your House' (Keeping
Current Matters, 29 February 2016), www.
keepingcurrentmatters.com/2016/02/29/
how-to-get-the-most-money-when-selling-your-
house, accessed March 2024

24 KCM Crew, 'How To Get The Most Money
When Selling Your House' (Keeping
Current Matters, 29 February 2016), www.
keepingcurrentmatters.com/2016/02/29/
how-to-get-the-most-money-when-selling-your-
house, accessed March 2024

25 KCM Crew, 'Why Pricing Your House Right
Is Essential' (Keeping Current Matters, 5
October 2020), www.keepingcurrentmatters.
com/2020/10/05/why-pricing-your-house-
right-is-essential, accessed February 2024

26 Stats presented by Tim Bannister at The Negotiator Conference, November 2023

27 Home Staging Association, 'The Home Staging Report 2023' (HSA, 2023), www.homestaging. org.uk/wp-content/uploads/2023/11/2023-HS-Report-Online-Version_compressed.pdf, accessed March 2024

28 Google Trends, UK Searches for 'home staging', 2019 to 2023, https://trends.google.com/trends/explore?date=all&geo=GB&q=home%20staging&hl=en, accessed March 2024

29 Home Staging Association UK and Ireland, *The Home Staging Report 2023* (HSA, 2023), www.homestaging.org.uk/wp-content/uploads/2023/11/2023-HS-Report-Online-Version_compressed.pdf, accessed February 2024

30 PhotoUp, 'Hot real estate photography statistics you need to know in 2024' (12 January 2023), www.photoup.net/learn/real-estate-photography-statistics, accessed February 2024

31 G Norwood, 'Most buyers won't read listings if they dislike photographs' (Estate Agent Today, 10 August 2023), www.estateagenttoday.co.uk/breaking-news/2023/8/most-buyers-wont-read-listings-if-they-dislike-photographs, accessed March 2024

32 FocalAgent, 'Want to sell properties 68% faster? Start using drone photography' (no date), www.focalagent.com/want-to-sell-properties-68-

faster-start-using-drone-photography, accessed
February 2024

33 I Stoughton, 'A standout video can help elevate
a property listing above the competition'
(Mansion Global, 26 May 2023), www.
mansionglobal.com/articles/a-standout-video-
can-help-elevate-a-property-listing-above-the-
competition-1615fd20, accessed February 2024

34 K Tan, '8-second attention spans and short
videos: The future of video-first marketing'
(Retail TouchPoints, 13 October 2023), www.
retailtouchpoints.com/features/executive-
viewpoints/8-second-attention-spans-and-
short-videos-the-future-of-video-first-marketing,
accessed February 2024

35 M Gladwell, *Blink* (Penguin Books, 2006)

36 A Kerr, 'Rightmove, Zoopla and the rest:
which is best?' (HomeOwners Alliance, no
date), https://hoa.org.uk/advice/guides-for-
homeowners/i-am-selling/rightmove-zoopla-
which-is-best, accessed February 2024

37 Rightmove, 'Our history' (no date), https://plc.
rightmove.co.uk/our-history, accessed March
2024

38 A Stone, 'Rightmove revenue up £27.7m on
2021 to £332.6m' (Directors Talk Interviews,
3 March 2023), www.directorstalkinterviews.
com/rightmove-revenue-up-27.7m-on-2021-to-
332.6m/4121108523, accessed March 2024

39 Statistic from YouGov poll commissioned
for internal use, the parameters used were:

'Profiles+ Great Britain 2024-03-03', target group 'buy/sell home in the next 12 months (n.11555)', target group description 'life events – next 12 months'.

40 N Whitfield, *The Ultimate Property Listing* (Independently published, March 2021)

41 Estate Agent Today, 'Five key ways that estate agents should be using social media in 2023' (7 January 2023), www.estateagenttoday.co.uk/ features/2023/1/five-key-ways-that-estate-agents-should-be-using-social-media-in-2023, accessed February 2024

42 B Dean, 'TikTok Statistics You Need To Know' (Backlinko, 15 February 2024), https://backlinko. com/tiktok-users, accessed March 2024

43 Today's Conveyancer, 'Upward trend in moves further from home' (18 December 2023), https://todaysconveyancer.co.uk/upward-trend-moves-home, accessed February 2024

44 'Proptech' is property technology – the use of IT to help companies research, buy, sell and manage real estate.

45 L Mody, 'The surprising way AI can help agents sell homes' (The Negotiator, 23 January 2024), https://thenegotiator.co.uk/blog-the-surprising-way-ai-can-help-agents-sell-homes, accessed February 2024

46 Madison Oakley, 'Who should do viewings - agent or owner?' (20 January 2011), www. madisonoakley.co.uk/2011/01/20/viewings-agent-or-owner, accessed February 2024

47   C Kannreuther, 'Do open houses work?' (The
     Savills Blog, no date), www.savills.co.uk/blog/
     article/192263/residential-property/do-open-
     houses-work.aspx, accessed February 2024
48   Select Committee on Office of the Deputy Prime
     Minister: Housing, Planning, Local Government
     and the Regions Written Evidence, 'Memorandum
     by the Office of the Deputy Prime Minister
     (AH 67)' (Parliamentary Business, 20 March
     2006), https://publications.parliament.uk/pa/
     cm200506/cmselect/cmodpm/703/703we79.htm,
     accessed 5 April 2024
49   S Cumbers, 'Divorce day 2024: statistics and
     insights' (Birkett Long Solicitors, 2 January
     2024), www.birkettlong.co.uk/site/blog/family-
     and-relationships/divorce-day-2024-statistics-
     and-insights, accessed March 2024
50   Commercial Finance Network, 'Demand
     for homes in rural areas rises due to the
     pandemic' (23 November 2020), https://uk-
     commercialfinance.co.uk/demand-for-homes-
     in-rural-areas-rises-due-to-the-pandemic,
     accessed February 2024
51   Lloyds Banking Group, 'Three years on: how
     the pandemic reshaped the UK housing market'
     (28 February 2023), www.lloydsbankinggroup.
     com/media/press-releases/2023/halifax-2023/
     three-years-on-how-the-pandemic-reshaped-
     the-uk-housing-market.html, accessed February
     2024

Acknowledgements

To my team at Lemon and Lime Interiors, thank you for your endless patience when I disappear to write.

Huge thanks to Simon Leadbetter for endless help to get the data right.

To my amazing network of fabulous estate agents, estate agent trainers, developers and clients who were so willing to provide quotes, wisdom and coffee throughout the process of writing this book, thank you.

To my family, especially Rob, thank you for the coffee, cake and encouragement.

To the amazing team at Rethink Press, thank you again for your support. This wouldn't have happened without you.

Also By Elaine Penhaul

Sell High, Sell Fast sets out the seven-step ADDRESS system that will enable you to realise your house's maximum value up to three times faster than comparable properties on the market.

'This is an absolute must-read for anyone selling property and looking to get the best possible price.'
— **Zahra Pabani**, Partner, Irwin Mitchell LLP

'*Sell High, Sell Fast* is a masterpiece of expert advice, straight from Elaine's own experience as a highly-respected, professional home-stager. She has been incredibly generous with her expertise and has presented it in an easy to access and informative format. A must-have for every home-mover.'
— **Jayne Dowle**, freelance homes and property journalist

'Elaine is one of a kind. Extremely experienced, diligent and professional, she is a source of invaluable knowledge, making *Sell High, Sell Fast* a must-read for anyone looking to deepen their understanding of how to sell their home well.'
— **Paloma Harrington-Griffin**, Founding Director of the Home Staging Association UK & Ireland and Vice President of the IAHSP® Europe (International Association of Home Staging Professionals Europe)

'Staging is so important for property marketing these days. *Sell High, Sell Fast* gives you insight to all the tricks to help you sell your home faster.'
— **Lee Armstrong**, Partner, Fine and Country

'*Sell High, Sell Fast* is a step-by-step guide to why, when and how to achieve amazing results by yourself or how to engage the services of a professional so that your sale stands the best possible chance of achieving the highest price in timely order. Great work!'

— **James Walker**, Director, Country Department, Savills (UK) Ltd

'*Sell High, Sell Fast* is everything your estate agent wants you to know about how to present your property in order to get great photos and video before you sell. Read it, it works!'

— **Martyn Baum**, Director, Martyn Baum Consultancy and former President of the National Association of Estate Agents

The Author

Elaine is passionate about property staging as a powerful marketing tool, and keen to debunk the myth of staging being a 'nice to have' service aligned with interior design. Her multi award-winning UK property staging business is utilised by agents such as Knight Frank, Savills and Fine & Country. She aims to help agents, developers and homeowners sell for offers up to 15% over guide price, four times faster than comparable unstaged homes.

Elaine is regularly quoted as a thought leader in property marketing. She has spoken internationally at venues from New Orleans to Brisbane and regularly features at UK events. She has been quoted in publications such as *Estate Agent Today*, *The Times* and *The Daily Telegraph* and contributes to many property podcasts. Elaine launched Stageflow, the first app to evidence return on investment for staging to a worldwide market and 2023 saw Elaine create the first UK training and coaching group for stagers, combining her earlier career in business coaching with her staging expertise. Her book *Sell High, Sell Fast* was published in October 2020 and immediately became an Amazon No.1 best-seller.

⊕ www.lemonandlimeinteriors.co.uk

▥ www.linkedin.com/in/elaine-penhaul-69aa8910

◎ @lemonandlimeinteriors